WHAT IS PROSPERITY AND DOES GOD WANT YOU TO HAVE IT?

Scripture Principles for Overcoming Poverty

Walter Hallam

Unless otherwise indicated, all Scripture quotations are taken from the King James Version of the Bible.

Copyright © 1997 by Walter Hallam

All rights reserved. Written permission must be secured from the publisher to use or reproduce any part of this book, except for brief quotations in critical reviews or articles.

ISBN #0-9661417-0-9

Walter Hallam
P.O. Box 1515
La Marque, Texas 77568

Contents

	Prologue 5
1	Tithing: Bread to Eat and Seed to Sow 9
2	Seed Time and Harvest 25
3	Half-Steps That Lead to Increase 41
4	Reasons Why God Wants Us to Prosper 55
5	Spiritual Answers to Spiritual Problems 71
6	Instructed to Prosper by the Holy Ghost 89
7	Give Bountifully, Not Sparingly 105
8	God Commands the Blessings Upon His People ... 115
9	The House of God: The Storehouse 127
10	Power to Get Wealth 141
11	What to Do First When You Enter the Promised Land 155
12	How to Turn It Around 169
	Epilogue 187

Prologue

God is moving throughout the earth today—so powerfully that His people must get ready for the changes that are involved with that. He is moving—sweeping through countries previously closed to the gospel...opening dynamic doors of evangelism in Russia and China and even the Islam nations. Gospel winds are blowing, and accompanying those gospel winds are winds of change.

The Holy Ghost spoke to me two years ago and said, "Walter, you will not recognize your ministry in two years' time—it will have changed so much!" Truly, the Lord has opened new doors of opportunity for this ministry—doors at TBN to enable us to preach the gospel to millions across the United States and in any country where there are satellite hookups...doors to take our soulwinning ministry into countries overseas...doors to take our message onto the late Lester Sumrall's satellite ministry, based in Honolulu, Hawaii. Yes, God is moving. And, true to His Word, this ministry has undergone drastic changes in recent months. While my wife, Cindy, and I are excited about what God has done through this ministry, we are even more excited about what He has in store for us—and for the body of Christ—in the days and months ahead. As we approach the year 2000, more sweeping changes are inevitable on earth as the Lord prepares the way for the promised return to earth of His Son, Jesus, and His long-prophesied Millennial Reign.

Yes, I am convinced that God has great things in store for His people in the days to come before Christ's return. But His people must be made ready. They must learn what it means to prosper and why God wants them to prosper. They must understand the heart of 3 John 1:2: *Beloved, I wish above all things that thou mayest prosper and be in health, even as thy soul prospereth.*

This and other related scriptures regarding biblical prosperity will be explored in-depth in these pages to make you ready to receive a great end-time outpouring of God's supply. As you will discover, there are a number of fixed, unchanging principles involved in being made truly prosperous in the Lord. We will examine these principles and learn how they may be applied in our daily walks with Him if indeed we are to experience His promise of abundant life. We will learn how to actually loose prosperity upon our lives through the power of the Holy Spirit.

We will learn that one of the reasons God wants us to prosper is that He simply wants to see us blessed. He's good. He loves us. He wants to bless us. And He wants us to prosper and have more than enough to meet our needs.

Finally, we will take a look at the number-one reason why God wants His people to prosper—soulwinning. God's heartbeat is for souls! And we are in the midst of the greatest harvest the earth has ever experienced. More souls can be reached today, in this era of amazing technological breakthroughs, than in any other time on earth. The possibilities for enhanced global communication are literally unthinkable...with the potential for soulwinning via television satellite and microwave signals expanding every day with mind-blowing speed. In the spring of 1995, for instance, Evangelist Billy Graham preached to one third of the world's total population with a single sermon that was televised via satellite uplink across several continents. Prior to this final decade of the twentieth century, that feat would have been not only impossible to achieve but impossible for a person to even comprehend. Yet such sweeping end-time evangelistic efforts were prophesied in the Bible: *And the gospel of the kingdom shall be preached in all the world for a witness unto all nations; and then the end shall come* (Matthew 24:14). Mark 13:10 states, *And the gospel must first be published among all nations.*

We *must* take the gospel everywhere: this command is not optional. God ordained it. The gospel *shall* be preached in all the world. *Then* the end shall come—the end, which is actually the beginning...the beginning of Christ's Millennial Reign on Earth.

If you already have a heart for souls, I pray this message will help you to understand how and why God wishes to place greater supply into your hands in this hour to take the gospel into all the earth. If you have seemed complacent regarding soulwinning, I pray that after reading this book, you will sense the fires of evangelism burning brightly within you as you come to a greater understanding of how God wishes to use you in this hour to reach lost and dying souls globally.

May the Lord richly bless you as you read and study God's Scripture principles for prosperous living!

1
Tithing: Bread to Eat and Seed to Sow

Today many people seem to have a lot to say on the subject of prosperity. Everyone wants to prosper—that's a fact. But there is more to the prosperity message than simply learning how to get it. We must also learn what to do with that prosperity, once it comes? What about God's purpose? What about His plan?

To be certain, God is moving in the earth today. There is a great shift beginning to take place in fulfillment of God's promise to place the wealth of the wicked into the hands of the just—His people's hands. This great transfer of wealth, in fact, is already beginning to take place.

Bankruptcies are at an all-time high. A lot of that money is winding up in church. Some of those who could once be considered "wicked" have found salvation and have brought great financial blessings with them into the house of God. But God is raising up great numbers of men and women who previously were not wealthy. The Lord is making them wealthy, and these individuals in turn will be great paymasters for this generation—men and women who have been prospered by God, understand what it means, and know how to give to get the work of the kingdom done on earth today. These individuals will be those used to help finance the move of God to take the gospel to this generation.

So all of this faith-teaching and all of this prosperity-teaching is not just to make you rich. If you come to church just intending to get rich, you will wind up sabotaging yourself and God's purposes for you. But if you fall in line with the principles of prosperity found within the Word of God, you will prosper. That *will* happen. But you will also find that money alone will not bring you true, lasting happiness. You must learn to use money God's way. In order to do that, you will need to know *why* God wants you to prosper.

The Word of God does not operate on laws; it operates on principles. As these principles are revealed to you, you will receive *rhema*—that is, a revelation of God's Word and it's deeper meaning. When you act on that *rhema* regarding your money, it is much the same as acting upon the spoken Word to receive salvation. Something happens. You begin to understand how God's economy works. You begin to understand how to use your money wisely. You begin to prosper.

God wants you to be blessed so you can do your part to help finance the move of God in this end-time generation. You are truly blessed to live in this generation, in a unique age when it is technologically possible to take the gospel to all four corners of the earth in virtually a single day. Right now, that can happen. The entire world is now in position to hear the gospel simultaneously either on shortwave, radio, the printed word, television, satellites, sonar—one way or other, the Word of God can go forth into all the earth if we can just tap into all those avenues available to preach the gospel.

In the days ahead, there will be churches raised up by God to tap into all these media resources now available. There will be single churches in the days to come that will preach to the whole earth in a single day. There will be churches that will go on satellite, get on radio, and print the word, blanketing the entire globe with the gospel message.

Lord, let my church be one of those churches! Let us become one of those power sources for the kingdom that You are busy raising up in this hour!

I can see in my spirit where we are headed as the body of Christ. It's bigger than a single sermon. It's bigger than a single book. There will be whole satellite networks devoted to disseminating the gospel. The whole world will be blanketed with the words of Jesus. Then the end will come.

There is plenty of work for everyone. Will you let God prosper you so you can do your part?

The principle of tithing

Much has been written on the subject of tithing as it pertains to prosperity. But this book is an in-depth study on biblical prosperity—not a "handy how to" book. After reading it, it is my hope and fervent prayer that you will not only learn how to prosper in the Lord, but *why* it is God's desire for you to prosper, and how to then wisely *steward* what He has so richly entrusted to you.

We must begin with the subject of tithing because tithing is so central to the issue of how to prosper in God. It is the cornerstone of all spiritual blessings pertaining to financial matters. To understand the vital link between tithing and prosperity is to understand God's system of supply and increase. To understand tithing is to understand with your Spirit-man that God wants your money to increase so that He can then teach you how to use it properly, according to the Word of God.

Lessons from childhood

When I was a little boy, my father made sixty-five dollars a week and raised seven children on that salary. He initially drove a laundry truck. My mama would get up at three-thirty in the morning and go deliver newspapers. She would get into a butane DeSoto and drive from Jasper, Texas, all the way to Livingston. She would be sick of the smell of butane by the time she got there. On Sunday mornings I rode with her. When she got to Livingston, she would pick up the *Houston Chronicle,* and we'd throw papers along the route home. When we got home, I'd take a little nap for about an hour, get up, get dressed, and go to nine o'clock Sunday school. That went on for years.

My mama and daddy taught the seven of us kids that the first dime of everything we earned was to be given to God. And today my mom and dad are not poor. God has blessed them over the years, and today they have every need supplied and plenty of money left over. They have prospered. And they taught their children how to prosper. They raised seven children, and not a single one of us is in a soup line today. Each of us still lives by the principle of tithes and offerings. Because Mama and Daddy understood what the Bible said about tithing, we were taught from childhood how to give to God and receive His increase.

That made it easy for Cindy and me when we were married in 1976. By the time we were married, I had saved enough to buy us a nice house-trailer. We worked together to outfit it with everything we could think of that we might need. When we moved in, we were all set to start our married life together. Right after we married, we got a new washer and dryer. (Even then, I knew enough about what it took to make a good marriage that I didn't want to put my new wife on a wash-board!) We had the same washer and dryer for seventeen years, and for all those years, we faithfully gave our tithes and offerings. So when that washing machine went out, we knew we'd gotten a lot of good use out of it. Cindy said, "Honey, can we buy a new washing machine?" I said, "You can buy anything you want. Just go pick it out and I'll pay for it."

But in the meantime, someone in our church came up to us after a service one day and said, "God said to buy you a new washing machine. I don't know if you need one or not, but God wants you to have one. So be home tomorrow at noon...and it will be there!"

There was a time when I might have said, "No, you don't have to do that!" But Cindy and I had been studying what the Bible has to say about prosperity. We had become familiar with the promise of Luke 6:38: *Give, and it shall be given unto you....* I said, "Thank you!" And the next day at noon, we had our new washing machine, compliments of God.

God has many different ways of causing finances to come into your life. He can either add it to the top, or take it off the bottom. It makes no difference—either way, you're blessed.

All God's thoughts toward us are good. He loves us. He wants the best for us. That includes prosperity; it is God's highest good for us. Isaiah 55:8 gives us excellent insight into God's heavenly thought patterns regarding mankind: *For my thoughts are not your thoughts, neither are your ways my ways, saith the Lord.*

Right there, we see that God's thought patterns are not the same as ours. His thoughts are subject to a different mode of operation than those of the carnal—or natural—man.

For as the heavens are higher than the earth, so are my ways higher than your ways, and my thoughts than your thoughts. For as the rain cometh down, and the snow from heaven, and returneth not thither, but watereth the earth, and maketh it bring forth and bud, that it may give seed to the sower, and bread to the eater: So shall my word be that goeth forth out of my mouth: it shall not return unto me void, but it shall accomplish that which I please, and it shall prosper in the thing whereto I sent it (Isaiah 55:9-11).

In these verses, we clearly see that God intends to use His Word to see that His plans for us on earth are accomplished down to the last detail. From this passage of text, we see that the Word of God that goes forth will do three things immediately:

- It will make things spring forth and bud.
- It will give seed to the sower and bread to the eater.
- It will accomplish that for which it was sent.

The producing power of God's Word

Anytime you plant a seed and that seed begins to bud forth, it's a sign of life. That seed may have looked dead for the entire winter, but when spring comes, tiny little green shoots will appear and begin to make their way upward from the dark, damp soil. That seed will begin to bud forth, and then you can say, "Oh, thank God, there's life there after all!"

Some of you may be in the winter of your lives right now—but I have good news for you! The Word of God will make you bud forth. Soon you will begin to produce fruit—the fruit of righteousness and prosperity. Why? Because God's Word says so...and His Word is infallible. It will do what God says it will do. When God's Word comes upon you, it will cause you to spring forth and to bud. And it will also cause two more things to occur.

It will give seed to the sower and bread to the eater.

I like to tell God I'm a bread-eater! The Word of God promises to give us enough bread to eat...with some left over to sow. Bread to eat...bread to sow. And God is not just talking about the kind of bread you buy by the loaf at the supermarket! He's talking about bread—symbolic of all those things in the natural that we need to sustain us, including the realm of finances. And He is talking about seed—not the kind you scatter on the ground to feed the wild birds or the kind you plant in the earth to get a cash crop—but seed as it applies to the seed we sow through tithes and offerings into the work of the kingdom. In Isaiah, chapter 55, God promises that His Word will supply both seed and bread.

Finally, God promises His Word will prosper. By that, He means it will grow up and become fully mature and perform His purposes in the earth as well as in our individual lives. One of those purposes is to rule both heaven and earth. God's Word prospers in that He is perpetually in control of all things. One of those purposes is to heal. Romans 8:2 states that *the law of the Spirit of life in Christ Jesus hath made me free from the law of sin and death.* There's evidence right there that God is a healing God! And according to Isaiah 53:5, *with his stripes we are healed.* Why? Because God's Word says so, and it always accomplishes what it was sent to accomplish, according to Isaiah 55:11. So every passage of Scripture, then, has its own purpose to accomplish. When we get a revelation of that fact, then we can be delivered from the law of sin and death, as stated in Romans.

Every scripture has a purpose—a specific task God intended it to perform. As you study the Word, it releases the anointing of God, and that anointing is like perfume. The very aroma of God begins to fill your life. Why? Because the presence of God is upon you, and you are becoming exactly like the Word. The Word of God has power. For instance, in 2 Timothy

1:7, God said He has not given us *the spirit of fear; but of power, and of love, and of a sound mind.* If you will learn to stand on that verse, you will discover that you are becoming more and more sound of mind...full of joy...full of love...and without any fear. Why? Because the Word of God accomplished in you what it was sent to do. If God said He did not give you a spirit of fear but of power, and of love, and of a sound mind, then because that Word has power, it will perform the purpose God intended it to perform—to make you sound of mind and full of love and free of fear.

If you had been studying 3 John 2, which says, *Beloved, I wish above all things that thou mayest prosper and be in health, even as thy soul prospereth,* you would soon find that you were beginning to prosper and enjoy improved health. And if you studied 1 Corinthians, you would learn, *Eye hath not seen, nor ear heard, neither have entered into the heart of man, the things which God hath prepared for them that love him. But God hath revealed them unto us by his Spirit...* (2:9,10). One of the necessities of the Holy Ghost is that He reveal to you and me the thoughts and ways of God. Otherwise, we'd be locked in carnality. Every time we face a problem, there is a carnal answer for it...and there is a spiritual answer. There is a natural way out...and there is a spiritual way out. In the natural, it may appear to be impossible, but God's ways are higher than ours, and with God all things are possible. His ways are completely different than our ways. The Scriptures are filled with examples of God's higher ways, pertaining to everything from salvation to healing to how to have a happy home.

But God did not just send scriptures that have to do with healing or salvation or a happy home. He also sent specific scriptures that have to do with our finances, and those scriptures are there for a reason. Why? Because He wants us to prosper as the Church, and as individuals. He wants us to be blessed and to increase.

It's all in God's Word

Notice again that Isaiah 55:10 begins with the words, "For as...". Then verse 11 begins with the words, "So shall...". Often in the Scriptures, you will find such word pairs used in parallel with one another. Anytime you see these pairs grouped together, God is saying, "The way *this* thing operates...is the way *that* thing operates." God will often use natural illustrations to explain spiritual principles. In this case, in Isaiah 55:10, He is saying that we are to take note of *how the rain falls to earth* and nourishes it. Then, in verse 11, we are to compare that phenomenon to the operation of His Word: *It shall not return unto me void.*

Dust to dust

When God created Adam, He formed him from the earth. Our human bodies are still made out of earth—a few pounds of chemical compounds mixed together with ninety-eight percent water. And the Bible is quick to remind us that it is to dust that our mortal bodies will once again return. When our bodies cease to function—if the Rapture does not occur by then—we will lay within our graves, and our bodies will deteriorate until they are no more than so many handfuls of chemical compounds—dust.

As descendants of Adam, we too are formed from the earth.

Thus, as with the rain falling to earth, God's Word will fall. It will fall on us and begin to water us, just as the rains water the earth. The water of His Word—cleansing water, life-producing water—has tremendous qualities. All of the qualities of life are contained within a single drop of the water of God's Word. When it falls on us and begins to water us, *it maketh it bring forth and bud...* (Isaiah 55:10).

That's what happens when the anointing of the Holy Ghost begins to fall! It begins to affect our lives. It begins to change things. It begins to change people. The man who was mean-spirited comes under the rain of the water of God's Word, and suddenly he no longer desires to be mean. The man who beat his wife sits under the cleansing water of the Word of God, and as it falls on him, he discovers that he no longer has the desire to physically abuse his wife. The Word begins to make people new. Why is that? Because Jesus is the **Word...*made flesh*...** (John 1:14).

One of my goals as pastor of Abundant Life Christian Center is to *drive poverty so far away from our congregation* that it will never again be upon the people of this flock. As people come here, I notice that many of them seem to be suffering from the same affliction—poverty...lack. But as they sit under the anointed Word as it goes forth, I've watched that curse break off them and have seen them begin to receive a new anointing—the anointing of provision. If they'll just begin to walk on the level of the Word of God and use the wisdom that comes from God, they will never again lack.

But that's what happens when a person gets serious about Jesus. When a person decides to follow after Jesus, He will make them different. Jesus said, *Follow me, and I will make you fishers of men* (Matthew 4:19). Another version of that verse says, "If you follow Me, I will REMAKE you." Time and again, I have seen this occur in individuals who have given their lives to Christ. They are REMADE by Him.

He will make us bud

For as the rain cometh down, and the snow from heaven, and returneth not thither, but watereth the earth, and maketh it bring forth and bud, that it may give seed to the sower, and bread to the eater: so shall my word be that goeth forth out of my mouth... (Isaiah 55:10,11). How powerful! Rain and snow, falling from heaven, set off a divine chain reaction of fruitfulness here on earth. The realm of nature is affected by this precipitation that falls from the heavens. But God is not talking about nature in this passage. He's revealing how the spirit-realm operates.

When the Word begins to fall on you, you will find that it is alive with life-producing properties, both spiritually and naturally. You will discover that God has begun to bring into being those things He originally created you to do. He will cause you first to bud, and then to bring forth fruit.

This principle reminds me of a television documentary I once saw on the Discovery Channel. It was about a desert. That desert was the driest, most parched piece of ground I had ever seen. It had big cracks running through it where the ground had become so dry, it had broken open. Some of those cracks were two or three inches wide—and an animal could easily have broken its foot just walking across that area. Nothing could grow there in that dry place. Then it began to rain. And when the rain fell on that dry and barren desert, the rain made the desert blossom and begin to bloom. I watched with amazement as brilliant-colored flowers began to spring up from that previously dry and parched soil. Grass began to grow. Everything began to spring to life when the rains fell.

God's Word is like that. When it begins to fall on your life, it will cause demons to flee...sickness to flee...weakness to flee...and it will make you spring forth and bloom, just like the plant life hidden in that desert. It will make you become what God always intended for you to be.

God's Word, however, is not like religion. It's not like psychology. I'm so tired of dried-up religion and worn-out philosophies. I don't want any part of those things. I want the water of life! I want that which Jesus himself spoke of—that water that cleansed lepers and made the blind see. I want that which Jesus will vindicate...that which terrifies demons. I want that which the god of this world cannot overcome...that which Jesus himself will always validate and confirm.

The Bible says when the Word of God falls upon you, it makes something begin to take place in your life. It *maketh it bring forth and bud, that it may give seed to the sower, and bread to the eater* (Isaiah 55:10).

The Word contains hope

Each time something begins to bring forth and bud, hope springs forth. A bud is a sign of hope—hope for tomorrow. It's a sign that there is something better coming up in just a few days. When the Word of God falls on you, the first thing that happens is this: you begin to *hope*. That hope—faith—comes from hearing the Word of God. After hope has budded, it will begin to bear fruit—the fruit of heaven. Whatever heaven has hidden in that one drop of water that just fell on you will begin to come forth and be made manifest—to be seen outwardly—in your life.

If you have been sick, the water of the Word will fall on you and cause your body to be made whole. If you have been having marital problems, when the water of the Word of God falls on you, you will come to understand that God created husbands and wives to walk in unity and that He is a restorer of families and marriages. You will learn that His is a message of reconciliation and that He can resurrect your love relationship.

When the water of the Word begins to fall on you, you will receive new ideas. Instead of turning and running from every problem, you will learn how to stand and speak to those problems as David spoke to Goliath. You will learn to look straight at that problem and say, "Today things are going to change!" Why? Because the water of the Word has begun to spring forth and bud in you. Now you have come under the influence of the Holy Spirit. Now you are becoming a different person.

Seed to the sower...

Verse 10 of Isaiah, chapter 55, says God will give *seed to the sower and bread to the eater*. The Word of God will do two powerful things: it will give you *seed to sow* and *bread to eat,* and God will bless those things.

Now we begin to get into the area of money.

As you are probably aware, the biblical tithe mandated in the Old Testament is a ten-percent, across-the-board gift of one's gross income to the Lord. That means when God blesses you with fifty or one hundred dollars, a tenth of that automatically belongs to God. That is seed—the tithe. If you have received ten dollars, one dollar of that belongs to God, and the remaining nine dollars belong to you. Those nine dollars are your "bread." They are to be used for yourself.

In these verses in Isaiah, chapter 55, God is saying that every word that proceeds from His mouth contains purpose. It contains promise. It contains the ability to produce. With each word of His mouth, God desires to make something on earth take place. And He says *it shall prosper.* God's Word, then, is literally loaded with the promise of prosperity. Every Word contains its own divine target. Every Word has its own purpose, and not a single word shall return to the Lord void of accomplishing that purpose. God sent each word for a reason.

And for those who will live on the level of the Word—pray it, stand on its promises, sit under it as it is preached—changes will occur in their lives. I've discovered that there is a simple principle at work here: "More rain...more growth. Less rain...less growth." God's Word is like rain from heaven, and it makes things grow in His children. It accomplishes its heavenly purposes in our lives.

That's why I get so excited when I read Isaiah 53:5: *...with his stripes we are healed.* I get excited about that scripture because just reading it, I know that God wants to heal somebody! He sent His Word so that when faith comes to believe it, you and I will be healed. I get excited when I read 2 Timothy 1:7 because by that I know that God expects me to overcome fear. It says, *For God hath not given us the spirit of fear; but of power, and of love, and of a sound mind.* I get excited when I read John 3:16: *For God so loved the world, that he gave his only begotten Son, that whosoever believeth in him should not perish, but have everlasting life.* I get excited when I read that because I know God wants to save somebody! He sent His Word so that when faith comes to believe it, a person can repent of his or her sins, receive forgiveness, and be born again.

I get excited when I read Acts 2:4: *And they were all filled with the Holy Ghost, and began to speak with other tongues, as the Spirit gave them utterance.* I get excited when I read that because I know God wants to fill somebody with His Spirit and give them the gift of tongues! He sent His Word so that when faith comes to believe it, a person can be baptized in the Holy Spirit and receive the gift of tongues.

And I get excited about Acts 1:8: *But ye shall receive power, after that the Holy Ghost is come upon you: and ye shall be witnesses unto me both in Jerusalem...and unto the uttermost part of the earth.* I get excited when I read that because I know God wants to fill me with the power of the Holy Spirit, then use me as a witness to the world! He sent His Word so that when faith comes to believe it, I can take the gospel to the uttermost parts of the earth.

God's Word contains promise, power, and purpose. It will not leave you the same as you were before you heard it proclaimed. It will change you. It will change your life.

Thus, after we read Isaiah 55:10 and 11, we know God's Word will accomplish that purpose for which it was intended. When we read 3 John 2, we know God's purpose is for His people to prosper: *Beloved, I wish above all things that thou mayest prosper and be in health, even as thy soul prospereth.* God sent that scripture for a reason. He sent it so that people would no longer be poor. One of those groups the gospel was preached to was the poor. If there were no poor people, there would have been no need for Jesus to preach the gospel. He came to preach the gospel to sinners. If there were no sinners, He would have had no need to preach to them—much less die for them.

So what is the gospel to a sinner? You don't have to live in sin! What is the gospel to a poor man? You don't have to live in poverty! Start living on the level of the Word, and it will make you to prosper. It will make you to spring forth and bud and produce fruit until the Word of God has performed in you the things it was sent to do.

Galatians 3:13-14 says, *Christ hath redeemed us from the curse of the law, being made a curse for us: for it is written, Cursed is every one that hangeth on a tree: that the blessing of Abraham might come on the Gentiles through Jesus Christ; that we might receive the promise of the Spirit through faith.* The promise of Abraham! Do you realize what that promise entails?

Prosperity! Abraham was not a poor man. In fact, he was the richest man on earth during his day. Prosperity was just one of many blessings of God that rested upon Abraham. Because of Christ, we can partake of these same blessings—and that includes prosperity.

But Abraham was a tither. He was a giver. He acknowledged God as his source and made regular offerings to Him. He knew the secret of giving—that it contained great increase. *Give, and it shall be given unto you; good measure, pressed down, and shaken together, and running over, shall men give into your bosom. For with the same measure that ye mete withal it shall be measured to you again* (Luke 6:38).

Give...and it shall be given

Some people think all preachers are interested in is money when they preach on tithing. But let me assure you, God doesn't need your money! Dollar bills don't work in heaven. That's not what tithing is about. It's not about buying your way into God's favor—it's about getting onto God's economy and receiving heavenly increase.

Some people are so bound up in greed that when they read Luke 6:38, all they can see is the word "give." So they give—once. But it's going to take a whole lot more than a one-time gift to get on God's economy. It's not about giving—it's about *getting*. The essence of this scripture verse is this: "Give, and it shall be *given* unto you."

When I read this verse, I no longer see the word "give." I see the words, "and it shall be given unto you." That is the key to understanding Luke 6:38.

Everyone likes to receive. I know I do. We serve a good God, and He likes to give to His people. So He says, "Give to Me one dime out of every dollar; keep nine for yourself. And I will take that dime and multiply it and give more back to you than just a dime." In the principle of tithing, God is trying to give to you—not get from you. Giving—that's how heaven operates.

How shall it return to you? Others will give to you. That's what Luke 6:38 states: men *shall...give into your bosom.* When we give, others will give to us—just like that man in our church was moved by God to give Cindy and me a brand-new washing machine. I get excited about that!

Still, some people have this mentality that God doesn't want them to have anything in life. They get hung up on a passage of scripture taken out of context, such as Mark 10:28, when Peter said, *Lo, we have left all, and have followed thee.* These people act like God is lucky to get their tithe. But that kind of giving—begrudgingly—won't do any real good. It will do absolutely no good to give God a tithe or offering with a wrong heart. That's like putting money in a bag with holes in it. The attitude of the heart must be right. God wants His people to prosper. He wants them to give willingly and freely—even cheerfully (see 2 Corinthians 9:7).

Only Jesus has the power to change your life financially. I think of the example of a couple in our church who came to us homeless. They were still living on the street when they began to attend services with us and to put into practice the Word as they heard it preached. Today they own their own home. No government program on earth could have done that for them, but Jesus could. He prospered this couple and changed their lives financially.

Big blessings come with persecutions

Let's go back to Mark, chapter 10. After reading Peter's remark about leaving all and following Jesus, the Lord said, *Verily I say unto you, There is no man that hath left house, or brethren, or sisters, or father, or mother, or wife, or children, or lands, for my sake, and the gospel's, but he shall receive an hundredfold now in this time, houses, and brethren, and sisters, and mothers, and children, and lands, with persecutions; and in the world to come eternal life* (vv.29,30)

There are some persecutions that come with receiving from God. Some people don't understand that concept. God says His ways are not our ways, nor His thoughts our thoughts (see Isaiah 55:6-8). He has His own method of doing things. He wants to bless us, but those blessings are not without persecutions. First Corinthians 2:9,10 states, *Eye hath not seen, nor ear heard, neither have entered into the heart of man, the things which God hath prepared for them that love him. But God hath revealed them unto us by his Spirit....* Some things come automatically when you start to obey God. Persecutions are included among those things. And some people can't handle them. They start giving the first ten percent of what they have to God. Then some old worldly person finds out about it and begins to say things like, "You mean to tell me that you give ten percent of everything you have to the church?" That gets into your spirit. That's persecution. Or perhaps family members will say, "You give ten percent of everything you make to the church? I can't believe it! Why, you must have been brainwashed over there at that church!" More persecution.

So it's assured in Mark 10:30 that persecutions will come —but when they do, rejoice because that means blessings are just around the corner. And the blessings are always greater than any of the persecutions that may come along.

Just stay on the level of the Word. Up there, where God's ways are higher than our ways and where His thoughts are higher than our thoughts, it says, "Give, and it shall be given unto you." Do that, and the Bible says you will be blessed. God is not trying to take your money—He's trying to give you more. He's trying to make you *the head, and not the tail...* (Deuteronomy 28:13).

In order to do that, He must do away with the poverty mentality many people had when they entered His kingdom. God wants His people blessed—blessed in the city and blessed in the field, blessed going out and blessed coming in (see Deuteronomy 28:3-6). If it can be found in the gospel and if it's a promise to prosper you, then you can count on it eventually coming to pass in your life. Why? Because God's Word cannot fail. It will always accomplish that for which it was sent.

And I get excited about that!

2
Seed Time and Harvest

God uses the principle of seed time and harvest to reproduce seed back into our lives. It is always accomplished through sowing and reaping, as farmers do. But there are both natural and spiritual principles at work in this concept of seed time and harvest. In Mark, chapter 4, Jesus tells about the seed and the sower and how the sower sows the Word, which is the seed:

> *...there went out a sower to sow: And it came to pass, as he sowed, some fell by the way side, and the fowls of the air came and devoured it up. And some fell on stony ground, where it had not much earth; and immediately it sprang up, because it had no depth of earth: But when the sun was up, it was scorched; and because it had no root, it withered away. And some fell among thorns, and the thorns grew up, and choked it, and it yielded no fruit. And other fell on good ground, and did yield fruit that sprang up and increased; and brought forth, some thirty, and some sixty, and some an hundred.*
>
> —Mark 4:3-8

In this important parable, we see that the seed falls on different types of ground. In good ground, the seed produces sometimes thirty, sometimes sixty, and sometimes a hundred fold. Sometimes the seed is eaten by the birds—thus, producing nothing. Sometimes the seed falls on stony ground and does not produce, and sometimes it falls among thorns that choke it out—signifying the deceitfulness of riches and the cares of this world.

Why do you want to prosper?

Check your motivations for wanting to prosper. It's always good to do that sort of inventory from time to time. If you want for yourself what God wants for you—prosperity, so you can give to God and help evangelize the earth—then you can't help but succeed. But if you want to prosper simply so you can build a big, new house, then you may be wanting to prosper for the wrong reasons. Don't get me wrong—God wants you to have a nice house. He wants you to drive a good car and have plenty of clothes to wear. We serve a God who is more than enough, and He wants you to have enough money to pay all your bills and have some left over.

But the devil doesn't want you to know that. He wants you to live on the level of fear, and he'll try to get you off tithing and giving offerings to God. He'll remind you of the bills that need to be paid and the braces the kids need on their teeth. He doesn't want you to eat the good of the land or understand the mysteries of seed time and harvest.

You must remember that only on good ground does the seed properly produce increase and multiply. Make sure your ground is good by observing the principles of seed time and harvest.

It all begins with a tiny seed

In another illustration, Jesus told a parable about the mustard seed. The tiniest of all seeds, when a single mustard seed is planted it has the potential of becoming a great, spreading tree that provides both shade and protection for the birds. Again we see the principles of multiplication and harvest.

Matthew 13:31-32 states, ...*The kingdom of heaven is like to a grain of mustard seed, which a man took, and sowed in his field: which indeed is the least of all seeds: but when it is grown, it is the greatest among herbs, and becometh a tree, so that the birds of the air come and lodge in the branches thereof.*

The devil doesn't want that tiny mustard seed to produce a great, spreading tree. That's why he'll do everything he can to place obstacles in the way of receiving a harvest from God. He'll try to put a mountain in the way. But even if your adversary is as big as a mountain, the Word says that as a believer, you can "speak to the mountain, and command it to be removed and cast into the sea." And that mountain is going to have to go! You can speak to the mountain, in the name of Jesus, with that small mustard-seed faith inside you, and that mountain will move—count on it!

So in teaching the principle of seed time and harvest, Jesus was not only teaching us the basics of farming. He was also teaching how the kingdom of God produces back into our lives, once we sow our tithes and offerings.

Greatness comes from sowing seed

Abraham did that, and God made him very, very rich. Isaac did that, and became very great, even during times of famine. Jacob did it, and the Lord blessed him and he, too, became great. David—once a simple shepherd boy—did it, and God made him king of Israel. His son Solomon did it, and God made him not only the richest man who ever lived, but also the wisest. The widow woman at Zarephath did it, giving the last of her provisions to God's prophet, Elijah. She sowed what she had, and reaped beyond anything she could have imagined. The Bible says that for the next three years, her barrel of meal and cruse of oil did not run dry.

Seed time and harvest. Get the vision for it, because when you first begin to plant your seed, things may look pretty barren. There may be nothing growing. But as you sow and reap and continue to do it, before long, you'll get a bumper crop. However, to reap big, you're going to need two things: patience and faith. You'll need patience because you'll always reap if you faint not. That implies a waiting period. Don't give up! And you'll need faith, in order to hang in there and keep believing you receive when things still look barren.

SEED TIME AND HARVEST ARE TWO SEPARATE SEASONS. One precedes the other. Jesus gives seed to sow and bread to eat. The sad part is that some people eat their seed.

Therefore, they can't have any harvest. On the other hand, one of the most joyful times is when you obey God and sow diligently and begin to reap the fruit of that obedience. You'll be planting while you're still reaping.

Greed will stop the crop

Greed interferes with living out the principles of seed time and harvest. So don't be greedy! If you're wrestling with greed, there is a solution. Malachi, chapter 3, tells how to break that off you. Here is what you need to do: Start tithing. When you do, that enmity in your heart against God and man will be broken down. Greed is usually motivated by fear and manifests itself as stinginess. Usually that is rooted in fear that there won't be enough to pay the bills. But remember—when Abraham began to tithe, he was full of fear because he had never given that much money away before. Immediately, the king of Sodom—representative of Satan—came to try to shake him off tithing. But Abraham stood fast, and then fear came over him. I am convinced that it's fear that keeps men and women of God from tithing. Tithing is critical. I don't believe you can give to God unless you first tithe. If you just make offerings, the Bible says you're cursed (see Malachi 3:9).

Perhaps as many as eighty percent of all Christians in America today fall into that category. The national average is around twenty percent for those who tithe—and these people are financing eighty to ninety percent of all church work on earth today.

In order to get that curse broken off, we must start tithing and then continue to walk in that. Eventually, we'll have a bigger harvest than we could ever imagine, once we get our thoughts and our ways in line with God's thoughts and His ways.

According to Deuteronomy, chapter 8, God wants you to have power to get wealth, so His covenant can be established in all the earth. He wants to use you—and me—to finance the kingdom of God on earth so that as He blesses you, you bless Him right back.

Genesis 8:21 says that when Abraham offered his tithe to God, *The Lord smelled a sweet savour; and the Lord said in his heart, I will not again curse the ground any more for man's sake....* What a beautiful scripture! Aren't you glad God lifted the curse? What a blessing!

Open heavens

Another promise given to us by God in Malachi, chapter 3, is that He will open the heavens to us. If we tithe according to God's Word, He promises we'll have "open heavens"—continual access to God in prayer, and continual access to receive His blessings and answers. He says if we'll just give our tithes and offerings, if we'll just give our ten-percent tithe and our free-will offerings above that, then God will rebuke the devourer for our lives and pour out blessings so bountiful that there won't be room enough to receive them all! Now, why would God want to bless us like that? So we'll get into position to begin to receive from Him and so that His will can be accomplished in our lives on earth "as it is in heaven."

God wants to open heaven's windows for us. He wants to pour out blessings so large that there won't be room enough down here on earth to contain them all. Now, I want that. I want God's will for my life to be done on earth as it is in heaven. How about you?

Jesus had something to say about that in the prayer in the Book of Matthew that has become known as "the Lord's Prayer." It's found in Matthew 6:9-13, and in it, Jesus says, *After this manner therefore pray ye: Our Father which art in heaven, Hallowed be thy name. Thy kingdom come. Thy will be done in earth, as it is in heaven. Give us this day our daily bread. And forgive us our debts, as we forgive our debtors. And lead us not into temptation, but deliver us from evil: For thine is the kingdom, and the power, and the glory, for ever. Amen.*

Now, that's a powerful passage of Scripture! You probably learned it in Sunday school, like I did. But I guarantee that in Sunday school, you and I did not come to the depths of understanding God intended us to have when applying this powerful prayer to our lives as Spirit-filled believers. There are some things He wants us to see here.

For one thing, we see again that God's thoughts are not our thoughts. They're higher. They're heavenly. When we begin to let the Word of God rain on us, our thoughts begin to change. They begin to become heavenly too, as we adopt the higher thinking patterns of our heavenly Father. We begin to be able to pray—and really mean it when we pray—"Not my will, but thine be done, Lord." That's what Jesus said we must do. Then as we pray, "Thy will be done," the words flow from our hearts and lips and something miraculous happens. We begin to take on the thoughts of God and to get a picture of His plan for our lives. Our own carnal plans begin to fall away in favor of God's larger, heavenly plan.

He's our Father, and He wants the best for His children. I began to get a measure of understanding for the heart of God when Cindy and I had our first child. Prior to that, I had only known the love of my earthly father as a son. I remember I used to go to my daddy and say, "Daddy, can I have twenty-five cents to get a Coke?" And he would say, "Yes," and hand me a quarter. I didn't earn that quarter, and I didn't have to do anything to receive it. All I had to do was to ask Daddy for it. He would just give it to me because he was my father and he loved me. I knew what it was to be a son and to have an earthly father who loved me. But I didn't understand what it meant to actually *be* a father. As I became a father, a strange new emotion was released inside me that I was totally unfamiliar with. Fatherhood added an entirely new dimension to my life. Immediately I realized that I wanted my children to have only the best—the best of everything, the best I could provide.

God is like that. He wants only the best for His children. He wanted that so badly that He was willing to sacrifice His best—His Son—for us so we could spend eternity in His presence. *He that spared not his own Son, but delivered him up for us all, how shall he not with him also freely give us all things?* (Romans 8:32). God gave His best gift—up front. So when you begin to pray God's will be done in your life, don't hesitate.

Never doubt that God will give you anything less than His best to meet the need you have right now in your life. When you pray, ask with the heart of a father. James 1:17 says, *Every good gift and every perfect gift is from above, and cometh down from the Father of lights, with whom is no variableness, neither shadow of turning.* Just think about it! God gives every good and perfect gift—every heavenly gift—to His children here on earth.

God is our Father. He's a rich God, and He wants His children to be just as blessed as He is. Just as we want a better lifestyle for our children than we have had ourselves, so God desires that His children have a higher standard of life than was possible after the Fall. If you're a parent, you know what it's like to be willing to sacrifice anything you have to sacrifice in order to see your children blessed. That's what God did for us. That's why He sent Jesus. He sent His best so we could be blessed. Jesus' agony on the cross and subsequent resurrection made all of heaven's resources available to mankind. It's called *grace.* He made grace available to you and me through His atoning work upon the cross. He made all of that—heaven's resources, grace, atonement—available to us so we could come up to a higher level and live according to a higher standard in life. In fact, Ephesians 2:6 says God *hath raised us up together, and made us sit together in heavenly places in Christ Jesus.* And God is saying, "I want you to see the riches of that inheritance in the life of the saints." He wants us to know all that has been made available to us in Christ Jesus. It's not less than what God has—it's all that He has.

So when we pray, "Our Father, which art in heaven," we need to get a revelation of what it means to have access to all that God has. It's called "a father's heart." The Father's heart will always give abundantly...and always give the best. As you get a revelation of that fact, you'll become immediately focused on heaven. And that will totally change how you pray. You will begin to get a picture of God's heavenly plan for your life, and of all the good things He has prepared for you—eternally, in heaven, and right here on earth. He doesn't want you to wait until you get to heaven to experience His goodness; He wants to pour some of it out on you right here! The Bible says there are streets of gold in heaven. It's hard to complain about all your earthly problems when you're praying to God, the Father, and focusing on heavenly things like streets of gold! Just think about heaven and focus on that, then see how your prayers will change in emphasis and scope. See how small those problems have become? Can you get a glimpse of God's perfect answers to those problems?

Now, when we pray, we must do so in the name of Jesus—*a name which is above every name* (Philippians 2:9). The name of Jesus is the sum of all power in heaven and earth. It is the sum of all the anointing, all the greatness, all the majesty. So when you pray, you need to pray in the name of Jesus. But you also need to thank God for His name because in addition to power, it contains promises. Another name for Jesus is *Jehovah Nissi*, and it means "the Lord our banner." Every time the devil comes and tries to do a number on you, you can call on that name and say to the devil, "See this flag? It's Jesus! He's my banner, and I am raising that name that is higher than any other name against you today!" And the devil will have no choice but to flee.

Another name for Jesus is *Jehovah Rapha*—the "revealed God," or "the revealing One whose person will be seen in healing." The word *rapha* actually means "health." In this name is contained the promise of healing because Jesus healed everyone who came to Him.

He is also *Jehovah Jireh*—"the Lord our provider." He provides all our needs abundantly. And He is *Jehovah Sidkenu*—"the Lord our righteousness," and "the Lord who makes all things new." He is the restorer—the One who has covered our sins and enabled us to stand upright before God, covered in His blood.

So when you pray, thank God for the name of Jesus. Thank Him for sending His Son to die for your sins and mine. Pray, "Thy kingdom come...." Then tell Him your problems and ask for His perfect solutions. He has a solution for each problem. But to receive those solutions, you have to access heaven.

Heaven is open to your cries when you tithe and give according to Malachi, chapter three. The heavenly kingdom is available to you, once you do that. In fact, Romans 14:17 tells us that the kingdom of God does not come in the form of *meat and drink; but righteousness, and peace, and joy in the Holy Ghost.* You need to call that kingdom into existence in your life. You need to start praying, "Oh, God, thank You for Your righteousness in my life today. Thank You for Your righteousness and for the kingdom of God coming into my life to rule it today. Thank You, God, that the kingdom of God will be manifested in every facet of my life today." The Bible says we're to call for the kingdom to come—"Thy kingdom come, thy will be done, on earth as it is in heaven!"

Is there any poverty in heaven? Not when the streets are paved with gold! If that poverty stuff tries to get on you, just start calling for the kingdom. Stated very plainly in Haggai 2:8 is the fact that God owns everything on earth: *The silver is mine, and the gold is mine, saith the Lord of hosts.* So if you need some of that gold and silver to take care of your needs in life, start calling on the name of Jehovah Jireh and let Him supply those needs by pouring a portion of those blessings into your life through those open windows of heaven.

Don't just sit back and take whatever comes along. Let me tell you something: "If you've just been living from paycheck to paycheck all your life, it's because you have disobeyed God with your money. God does not want His people living from pillar to post...hand to mouth. He said, "I will bless you and you will be a blessing." In Genesis 12:2, God stated that very plainly. How can you be a blessing if God has not first blessed *you?*

You are blessed, not cursed! He has redeemed you from the curse (see Galatians 3:13), and contained in that curse were poverty and lack. Learn to think like God thinks. Learn to have a heart like God's heart.

If you have children, then you understand what I'm talking about. As parents, you begin to enter into understanding the heart of God the Father. It involves all the emotions and tenderness we feel as human parents...and goes far beyond.

We should have the heart of the Father. That's something to rejoice over. But there are a few other things to rejoice over as well....

Four things to rejoice over

Having the heart of the Father should cause you to rejoice, and so should having the heart of the home, which is heaven. And in your prayer life, you should thank God for that fact. It's cause for rejoicing.

Another thing to rejoice over is what I call "the God-kind of heart." It's the kind of heart that says, "Thy kingdom come!" and means it. It's the kind of heart that focuses on the kingdom lifestyle. This Spirit-filled life is not an experience—it's a lifestyle. When we pray, we need to focus on that kingdom lifestyle, with "the God-kind of heart." It will produce in us a cause for rejoicing. It will produce love for others. It will produce wisdom and understanding. It will produce the character of godliness, and it will control you to such an extent that it will literally break all other forms of control off you.

Finally, you should develop the heart of God in prayer, if you plan to walk in prosperity. By that, I mean that the will of God must literally become your vision and your desire. You must ask God to reveal His will for your life, and then get the vision for it deep down in your heart. Even when the pressure hits, you must not come off that vision. Hold fast to it, and say in prayer, "Thank You, Lord, that I am fulfilling the desire in my heart that Jesus of Nazareth placed inside me!"

You don't have that on the inside of you yet? Well, do you want it? If you do, then it's as simple as telling God, "Yes, I'm willing and obedient. I will have the will of God, the desire of God, the vision of God, and the manifestation of God performed in my life, and I'll be a doer of His will." Then watch what happens as God first fills you with purpose and vision, then brings those things to pass in your life—before your very eyes.

And that's just one more cause to rejoice!

By that time, every demon in hell will complain of migraine headaches because you'll be praying in line with the will of God—and nothing can stop that kind of prayer from being answered! That kind of prayer echoes through the corridors of heaven and rumbles through the caverns of hell. Mixed with faith and prayed according to the will of God, that kind of prayer makes the devil put his hands over his ears and moan, "Make him stop! He's praying like Jesus—'Thy kingdom come, thy will be done...on earth, as it is in heaven!'"

Give, forgive, lead, deliver...

Now, there are four areas I want you to look at, regarding the Lord's Prayer. I refer to these areas in shorthand: "Give us," "Forgive us," "Lead us," and "Deliver us." These four areas are very powerful in prayer. These were four areas Jesus talked about. Notice that God wants us to prosper—so much so that He leads off the Lord's Prayer with the petition, "Give us our daily bread...."

Please understand the context in which Jesus was praying. Here was a man whose thoughts were focused completely on God. He had the vision, and He understood God's ways totally. He knew that if He brought His needs before the Father, He would receive all that He needed from heaven. He was, in effect, saying, "This is what I need today, Father, in order to get heaven's business done on earth. These are the things I need down here in order to accomplish what You have called me to do for You. My daily bread...."

So by that, we see that it's perfectly all right to talk to God in prayer concerning our physical, material, and financial needs. Jesus doesn't want you to be poor. If you need money, ask! Just make sure you use that money to pay your bills, because Christians pay their bills. We don't duck when we see the shopkeeper coming. We can hold our heads high and look him right in the eye. We pay our bills and meet our obligations, so there is no need for embarrassment over money. We pray... and then we pay.

So if there are some things lagging behind—some bills that need to be paid—it's perfectly all right to offer them before the Lord and ask Him to help you pay them off. Just say, "Lord, I'm asking You to give me what I need today to help me pay off these obligations." Are there other things you need? A car? A job? Ask! God wants you to have those things, and He is well able to provide them.

Then He says, "Forgive...."

If you have committed any sin that shades your heart from God, you need to say immediately, "Lord, forgive me!" But it goes beyond just that. You must also forgive those who have wronged you, saying, "Lord, I forgive them." In so doing, you are repenting—turning and going the other way. You are turning from unforgiveness and turning toward walking in the full forgiveness of God and man. You turn from sin, and you turn from the guilt produced by it. Jesus included this petition of forgiveness in the Lord's Prayer because He knew how important forgiveness is to us on earth.

Next He leads us. Thank God for that fact! Psalm 119:105 says, *Thy word is a lamp unto my feet, and a light unto my path.* That's what we need—direction. And no one can provide that quite like the Holy Ghost. He leads us by His Spirit. He leads us by speaking through an anointed preacher or teacher of the Word. He leads us through the pages of the Bible. He leads us at times by speaking to us. In powerful ways, He leads His people. We have an unction from the Holy One, and it leads us. John 10:27 says, *My sheep hear my voice....* He leads us.

He also delivers us. He delivers us from evil. Aren't you glad that we serve a God who delivers us? You can also rejoice because God will never lead you into sin. He will walk with you through the valley of the shadow of death, as promised in Psalm 23, but He won't ever lead you into sin. He will lead you through His Word and by His Spirit, but never into sin. You won't have to fear the evil all around you because Psalm 91 promises that it won't come near you.

Praise God for the powerful images and promises contained in the Lord's Prayer! There is a kingdom revealed there, and it will rule your life if you will let it. The Lord wants you to know there is a vision for your life, a plan, and a desire. And when those things are established in your life, all you need to pray is, "God, give me those things I need to see all these visions and plans brought into existence."

"Give us this day our daily bread." I like to remind God about that part because when I do, I realize how impossible it is to ever bankrupt heaven. Its supply is eternal and endless. First Corinthians 2:9,10 says, *Eye hath not seen, nor ear heard, neither have entered into the heart of man, the things which God hath prepared for them that love him. But God hath revealed them unto us by his Spirit....* As I have prayed according to the Lord's Prayer, the Holy Ghost has shown me some things about my tomorrows—and I'm excited about that. Sometimes when I think about those tomorrows, I begin to feel like David—like I could run through a troop, jump over a wall, or slay a lion, all in the name of Jesus. Why am I excited about those tomorrows? Because the Word says, *The path of the just is as the shining light, that shineth more and more unto the perfect day* (Proverbs 4:18).

One day, a new heaven and a new earth

One day God is going to renovate the globe by fire. In that one day, the whole planet will be destroyed, and a new heaven and a new earth will emerge. But that day will take place only after the Rapture, when the Lord lifts His people out of here. Then the seven-year tribulation period will take place—and at the end of that, the planet will be purified by fire. Jesus will return and preside over an unprecedented thousand-year period of peace. He will physically rule planet earth. Praise God!

At the end of Christ's millennial reign, the devil will again be loosed on earth for a short season. But, once again, Jesus will defeat him—and this time, the devil's permanent destination will be the lake of fire. He'll spend the remainder of eternity there, along with his fallen angels. And we will spend the remainder of eternity with Jesus, in His new Jerusalem, the city of heaven.

Now, that may kind of ruffle your feathers, but until the day Jesus renovates the earth by fire, this planet isn't going anywhere. No matter what the scientists say, no matter what the literature and scientific publications say, earth is here to stay ...until that moment when the Lord sends fire.

God's promises about the seasons

Until that time, Genesis 8:22 states, *While the earth remaineth, seedtime and harvest, and cold and heat, and summer and winter, and day and night shall not cease.* This was spoken by God to Noah after the flood, when He commissioned Noah and his family and all the animals to go forth and repopulate the earth. During the flood, many things about earth and its atmosphere were changed. For instance, prior to the flood, the skies did not contain rain-bearing clouds. Prior to the flood, earth was surrounded by mist and watered itself. But after the flood, there were periods of rain, followed by dry periods—sometimes even drought.

God said as long as the earth remained, these seasons and changes in weather patterns and the distinctions between day and night would remain. So I don't care about what the scientists say about global warming—it's not the threat they say it is. They're operating out of the philosophy of the age, not the spirit of truth. Man cannot destroy what God has created, no matter what fear-doctors may get up and preach. Just a few years ago, the rage was fear of nuclear proliferation, global warming, or an impending ice age. But God said there would always be summer and winter, cold and heat. And that's how it will be on earth until Jesus comes back, renovates the planet with fire, and once again changes the natural order of life on this planet.

The "doomsayers" are misinformed!

Some believe this is the "terminal generation." But the doomsayers are misinformed. It's not the "terminal generation"—it's the end time. And that's different. Actually, that's good news because it means Jesus is coming soon, and we're going up in the Rapture before things get really bad down here.

However, I'm not advocating trashing out the planet. Simple good stewardship of planet earth means that if you throw down a piece of trash, you should pick it up and dispose of it properly. You should not pollute the water or the atmosphere. That's just taking care of the planet through good stewardship. But just know that the planet isn't going anywhere any time soon, so there's no cause to be caught up in the various fear doctrines being promoted by the scientific community.

And if we're going to be here until Jesus comes back, we might as well occupy the planet until He comes. We might as well advance the gospel, win souls, and promote the kingdom. If the heart of God is souls, then we might as well focus our efforts on soulwinning and evangelization. People can't get saved unless somebody tells them about Jesus, so we might as well do that.

If we don't do that, the devil will rule. Cults will rule. Deception will rule. False religions will rule. Lies will rule. Scientific fear doctrines about global warming and environmental doom and gloom will rule. So if we love God, we might as well occupy the earth until Jesus comes.

Occupy until He comes

For some of us, that will entail breaking some habits. For some, it will mean breaking out of a routine of doing nothing. For some, it will mean rising up and becoming active in church and ministering to the community. Every believer is called to witness for Jesus, and that simply means we are to share the gospel. This is no time for people to just sit back and do their own thing. Jesus wants everyone to do his or her part in these critical end times.

3
Half-Steps That Lead to Increase

I thoroughly believe that anyone who applies God's Word pertaining to prosperity will see his or her financial situation turn around eventually. It's not like following a few handy steps—step one, step two, step three. It's more like *taking* steps—a series a small half-steps with God as you learn to understand and operate within His principles.

The God who promotes

God is a God of promotion. He is a God of increase. Yet there are many Christians on earth today who have never understood God's nature pertaining to increase and promotion. Consequently, they are living far beneath the best that God has stored up for them. Wonderful things are available—just waiting for them to get understanding and begin to access all that goodness.

If there is one thing I know for certain about God, it's this: He wants us to develop a lifestyle of giving. If we will do that, He will promote...and promote...and promote. He will bring us forward again and again through a series of small half-steps.

Why not giant leaps? At times, it may seem that someone has made one or two giant leaps forward. But upon close examination, we are able to see the series of half-steps that led up to what appeared to be that giant leap forward. God's promotion is gradual.

I was reminded of this fact one day while watching a maintenance man change a light bulb high up in our sanctuary. He was at the top of one of those big, tall ladders. I became fascinated, watching him work so high above the ground. Then the Holy Ghost began to prompt me to really pay attention.

Suddenly I began to notice several things that I might otherwise have disregarded. I noticed, for instance, that the steps on that big ladder were between sixteen and eighteen inches apart.

Now, this was a rather large man. Yet he wasn't taking great big, giant steps on the way up that ladder. Instead, he was taking small half-steps. I was thinking, *If that guy misses one of those little half-steps, he could quickly wind up at the bottom of the ladder.* That's when the Lord began to talk to me about His way of using half-steps forward in promoting His people.

"It's the same way spiritually," the Lord said to me. He revealed that serving Him is not according to one great feat or a single giant leap—but by a constant series of half-steps. And He pointed out that on the way up, a person may take smaller steps—and more of them—than he would if he were just moving along laterally. Why? Because as you go up higher, the going gets a little precarious.

But it's those little half-steps that will eventually get you to the top. Half-steps of prayer. Half-steps of praise and worship. Half-steps of walking by faith. Half-steps of daily Bible reading. Half-steps of meditating on God's Word. Half-steps of thinking upon the things of God.

Sometimes a little half-step forward can be as simple as turning the dial off that secular radio station and tuning into a Christian station. There it is—in that one small half-step, your entire mindset is changed for the entire day so that when the devil attempts to come against you later, he will find no place to lodge an attack.

Or perhaps it's that small half-step of turning the channel on the television—away from some program you know you shouldn't watch...to something that is more pleasing to God.

Maybe it's that half-step you took when you refused to allow evil to be spoken about someone else in your presence ...or when you spoke positively about someone when they were not present to hear.

Half-steps.

People would speak more carefully if they just realized that sometimes a single conversation could set them back as much as five years, spiritually. Conversely, there are those who are set back spiritually by what they have heard. That thing that offended them, due to some weakness in their own character, took root and set them back. So they lost ground spiritually and back-tracked.

Half-steps run in both directions—toward the things of God...and away from them.

It's the same as training children

If you have raised children, you know the importance of training them in small half-steps. "No, you can't sass Mommy and Daddy." "No, you can't do whatever you want; you're going to learn to love God and live virtuously." "No, you can't back-talk your brothers and sisters!"

If your children are ever going to learn these things, they will have to learn them at home—from you. And each one of those half-steps of training are necessary in order to raise your children correctly. Every small step is important.

It's important that you don't skip over one of these steps in training your children. And it's equally important that you don't leap over any of God's principles. Half-steps. Keep on living them. Keep on doing them. Keep praying. Keep fasting. Keep giving as the Spirit of God blesses you. Keep paying off those nasty credit card debts. Keep one or two cards, but get rid of the rest of that plastic.

Half-steps. I began to ask the Lord for wisdom regarding these little half-steps. I prayed, "God, show me the half-steps to spiritual and financial success."

The miracle of the loaves and fishes

Let's look at Mark 6:31-34. In this passage of Scripture, Jesus is speaking to the apostles:

> *Come ye yourselves apart into a desert place, and rest a while: for there were many coming and going, and they had no leisure so much as to eat. And they departed into a desert place by ship pri-*

> *vately. And the people saw them departing, and many knew him, and ran afoot thither out of all cities, and outwent them, and came together unto him. And Jesus, when he came out, saw much people, and was moved with compassion toward them, because they were as sheep not having a shepherd: and he began to teach them many things.*

The first thing the Lord spoke to my spirit regarding this text was this: "If you are going to minister, you must take time to rest!" Today there are many seminars about how to get rid of stress. But there is a better way to get de-stressed than to pay a lot of money to attend a seminar. Why not put that money in the offering plate at church and go somewhere private and quiet and put a teaching tape into the cassette deck? As you listen to the Word of God as it goes forth, you'll feel that stress beginning to leave you. Stress is not a mental problem. It can be a very strong spiritual problem—but, thank God, Jesus of Nazareth can lift that heavy yoke off and replace it with a light and gentle yoke.

Next we see that even though He was tired and had not yet been able to rest, Jesus saw the crowds pressing near, had compassion on them, and began to teach them. Verses 35-42 tell us what happened next:

> *And when the day was now far spent, his disciples came unto him, and said, This is a desert place, and now the time is far passed: Send them away, that they may go into the country round about, and into the villages, and buy themselves bread: for they have nothing to eat. He answered and said unto them, Give ye them to eat. And they say unto him, Shall we go and buy two hundred pennyworth of bread, and give them to eat? He saith unto them, How many loaves have ye? go and see.*
>
> *And when they knew, they say, Five, and two fishes. And he commanded them to make all sit*

down by companies upon the green grass. And they sat down in ranks, by hundreds, and by fifties. And when he had taken the five loaves and the two fishes, he looked up to heaven, and blessed, and brake the loaves, and gave them to his disciples to set before them; and the two fishes divided he among them all. And they did all eat, and were filled.

There you have it—one of the Bible's classic miracles of God's ability to supply!

Jesus knew about half-steps

First, Jesus divided up the huge crowd into smaller groups so it would be easier for the disciples to minister to them. No big spiritual principle at work here—just common sense. It doesn't take a rocket scientist to figure out that it's easier to minister to eighty-five people than to thousands all at once. Jesus knew exactly what He was doing. Half-steps. He knew what He wanted to take place, and He knew what was necessary in order to make that happen.

I'll tell you one good half-step to success that you can start doing right now: balance your checkbook regularly! You should know at all times—right down to the penny—how much money you have in your bank account.

Jesus asked His disciples for an accounting of their resources that day. How many loaves? How many fishes? It's the same with the resources in your bank account. You should know what is there at all times. After all, you're responsible for stewarding it.

After the disciples brought the loaves and fishes to Jesus, He lifted them to heaven and blessed them. Then He broke them...and began to divide the pieces also. Half-steps. He didn't look down at the meager supply and then out into the hungry faces of the multitude. He looked up—toward heaven—and blessed what He held in His hands.

Have you ever had more "month" than money? Have your monthly bills totaled more than you had in the bank? Well,

Jesus can sympathize. He had five thousand men—plus their wives and families—to feed that day. That means there were probably fifteen to thirty thousand people gathered there on the hillside, waiting to be fed. Often it may seem that you have a lot to attend to. There may be great necessity placed upon your finances, and you don't have as much money in your bank account as you need to pay out. Why not take a look at what you do have, then lift up your resources to heaven? Start thanking God for what you have instead of grumbling about what you *don't* have. Half-steps.

Even if you just have five mouths to feed, at times it may seem like five thousand—especially if you have teenagers at home. Each time you're tempted to sit down and say, "Dear God, how am I going to do it?" why not sit down and look toward heaven, then thank God for what you have.

Notice what Jesus did in Mark, chapter 6: He offered God what He had. He gave it to God. Then He blessed it and, in effect, said, "We'll go as far as we can with this thing." One day as I studied this passage in Mark, chapter 6, the Holy Ghost spoke to my spirit and said, "Don't ever be moved by the size of the task in front of you versus what you have in your hands to work with."

You might say, "But I have fourteen thousand dollars' worth of bills and only nine dollars and eighty-seven cents in the bank!" Here's what you do: Take that nine dollars and eighty-seven cents and give it to Jesus. Tithe ninety-eight cents of it, and see what God will do with what's left. Watch Him multiply it into that fourteen thousand dollars you need—with some left over—and give you wisdom to handle every little piece that you start breaking off.

First, tithe!

It may appear that you don't have enough money to go around. First, tithe! First, give ten percent to God. Even if you don't have enough money to pay your bills, offer what you have to God—and tithe on it. Then prioritize what you have to pay. Some things are necessities in life, and some are commodities.

First, tithe. Then pay the necessities. If you have foolishly loaded up on the commodities and are now having to deal with that, start working to change that lifestyle today. You don't have to continue that way. Deal with the necessities and put the commodities on restriction.

With what is left over, start paying off the commodities. Don't try to maintain an opulent lifestyle. Do what you can do —stay faithful...pray...tithe. Then see how God will take what you have and cause it to begin to stretch...and stretch...and stretch...until it covers far more ground than you could have covered on your own. It's incredible how fast those bills will start falling off you, once you make the decision to pay them off and stop making new ones for things you don't need.

God will do two things when you tithe to Him and give offerings: First, He will multiply what you have. Secondly, He will take away that which is eating at you. He can cause you to increase from both sides. But first, you must line up with God's half-steps to success.

Mark 6:42-44 states, *And they did all eat, and were filled. And they took up twelve baskets full of the fragments, and of the fishes. And they that did eat of the loaves were about five thousand men.*

Ever wonder what Jesus did with those twelve baskets filled with the leftover fragments of loaves and fishes after the thousands were fed? The Bible doesn't say, but I like to think that He gave it all back to the boy who had so generously given up his lunch. I can just see Jesus saying to the boy, "Just give Me what you have." Then I can see his eyes grow wide with wonder as he watches the Lord lift that meager lunch skyward, bless it, then begin passing it throughout the crowd. Imagine the boy's amazement when he saw how far that small lunch stretched that day! A miracle—that's what it took to feed thousands of hungry mouths on the hillside that day.

But imagine also—that small boy gave away everything he had. To be certain, he was as hungry as anyone present. His stomach may have even growled as he gave his lunch over into the Lord's hands. Yet he obediently relinquished what he had, and God blessed it and used it to perform a great miracle. Half-steps.

Principles of success

There are several things I call *principles of success*. If you learn them and do them, you will have success. While we are on the subject of half-steps of success, it would be good to discuss these principles. They are actually half-steps in and of themselves. Learn to incorporate them into your walk with God, and, in time, you will reap wonderful results.

Find Scriptures that promise answers.

In the verses we've just studied—and in Isaiah 55:10,11 that we studied in chapter one—we can clearly see that God's Word contains both power and purpose. It has power to accomplish miracles, and it will not return to God void. If the Word of God says He will cause a thing to prosper, then you can be certain it will prosper. Thus, if the Word of God promises you financial prosperity, you can be certain your finances will prosper because God desires that you prosper.

First John 5:14,15 says: *And this is the confidence that we have in him, that, if we ask any thing according to his will, he heareth us: And if we know that he hear us, whatsoever we ask, we know that we have the petitions that we desired of him.* I get pretty excited about these verses because they clearly state that if we ask anything according to God's will, He will hear and answer. We can have confidence in that fact. But asking according to His will involves much more than simply asking that which is God's will for our lives. It's also a matter of God's will for asking. By that, I mean it is His will for us to ask.

In the Psalms, David expressed his delight in doing the will of the Lord. In Psalm 119:11 he wrote, *Thy word have I hid in mine heart, that I might not sin against thee.* The *will* of God and the *word* of God are synonymous. That being the case, if we ask anything according to His will, then we understand that it means to ask anything according to His Word. And if we do that, He hears us.

Now, listen real good: God doesn't want to give you a little cabin in the corner of glory-land. Stop praying those little cabin-in-glory-land prayers! Start asking God according to His will...according to His Word. The Bible says His will is that you may prosper and be in health, even as your soul prospers (see 3 John 1:2). Think big! Ask big! He's a big God. Expect big answers! Start talking to God the way the Word of God talks to you!

Why would you even want to ask God for something that's not in line with His will for asking? God never says you should be content with asking things like, "Oh, God, just give me enough to get by!" Stop praying those get-by prayers! God never said anything like that. Yet when I hear people say things like that, it just goes off in my spirit. I can't stand to hear it. "If You just give us enough to get by, we'll be happy!" *You will not! You're just getting by now, and you're by no means happy!* Why not start asking God according to His will for asking? Ask big, according to God's promise in Philippians 4:19: *But my God shall supply all your need according to his riches in glory by Christ Jesus.* Get up on the level of God's Word; then ask big, believe big, and receive big answers.

If you want to find the will of God for asking, learn the Word of God. Then pray it. Get in the Word, and before long, you'll know exactly what the will of God is for your life.

Continue in the Word.

In John 8:31,32, Jesus said, *If ye continue in my word, then are ye my disciples indeed; and ye shall know the truth, and the truth shall make you free.* Once you have established the Word of God in your life—once you study it, pray it, and learn to walk in it—*continue in it.* Believe it. Become His disciple—a "disciplined one, one who lives a structured life." I'm talking about a lifestyle of holiness, a lifestyle of the Word, a lifestyle of faith, a lifestyle of continuity in the Word. Jesus said if you continue in the Word, you will be His disciple *indeed,* and *then* you shall know the truth and it shall make you free.

That causes me to understand that although we hear and do the things of God, it may yet be some time before we actually have a revelation about some of those things. Revelation may come later, after we've walked in the Word for awhile. Yet even without a revelation, we must continue in the Word.

For example, have you ever read a scripture verse hundreds of times, then suddenly one day receive *rhema* on the inside of you to understand it in great depth and detail? It's the same with any of God's principles. Although you may not fully understand why they are important, do them; continue in them. Tithing, laying on of hands, praying, praying for the sick, praying in tongues—continue in those things. The process is progressive. It continues to unfold...and unfold...and unfold. And when you do that, the Bible says you will be made free. Free of what? Disease, sin, poverty, fear, old religious dogma.

To those who believed, Jesus said, *Continue in my word.* He is still saying, *Continue in my word.* Obey.

Use wisely what God has given to you.

Pray over your money. Use what you have wisely. If you don't have a plan for your money, ask God to give you a plan. Ask Him to give you a plan for your finances. Now, I'm no perfect example, but I can give you a few examples from mine and Cindy's lives to illustrate what I mean. As I have already explained, Cindy and I were all set up in a brand-new house-trailer when we married. I purchased it while working for Louisiana Pacific as a purchasing agent. I did all the buying for a big sawmill—including handling all of the payroll. It was a pretty good job for a young man of twenty-two. In 1976, Cindy and I were just kids, but we had enough wisdom to realize that if we planned well and worked hard, we could avoid the pitfalls of heavy debt.

I remember buying that fourteen-by-seventy-six-foot house-trailer. The payment was $117 a month, and I remember thinking, *Oh, God—how are we ever going to do it? A hundred and seventeen dollars a month is a whole lot of money!* But we bought it and set it up six months before we were married. Then

Cindy and I began to fill it up with every conceivable thing we could think of that we might need, once we were married. We stocked it with groceries. We loaded it up with small appliances and dishes and trash cans—right down to the toothbrushes. We had that thing fully stocked so that, once we were married, we could come back from our honeymoon and move right in, totally set up.

The point is, by the grace of God, we used wisdom and never got ourselves into a hole financially. We made the decision not to get in over our heads. I'll never forget that at our wedding, my daddy gave us a one-hundred-dollar bill. Then he said, "Son, don't spend it all in one place." Now, he could have given us more than that, but he had already given me twenty-two years of understanding and expertise and training. He would have given me more money if I had needed it, but that isn't even the issue. The issue is that he gave me that hundred-dollar bill and said one more thing: "Bless God, if I've done a good job as a daddy, that's all I'll ever have to give you from this day forward!" And it was! From that day to this, Daddy has never had to give me another dime.

Cindy and I made a decision at the very beginning of our lives together that we were not going to go out and get ourselves into hock over things that would just wear out anyway. We decided to plan for the things we would need, and then save money so we could pay for things we acquired.

In addition, we tithed to our church, which also happened to be my father's church. Every week when our paychecks arrived, we took the first ten percent right off the top and gave it to the church. We wrote out a check to cover ten percent of the gross and put it in the offering plate, then thanked God because we had it to give, and that every bill was paid.

It started right there, that long ago. We also started a little savings account. If you don't have one, get yourself a savings account started. Learn to save as well as to pay out. If this thing called biblical prosperity works—*and it does*—you'll need a savings account because you'll have more than you can spend. Don't get greedy and try to make a mega-jump to a different level of lifestyle. Just stay put, save, plan, tithe, give, and watch what happens. Keep walking in those little half-steps.

Before long—maybe in six months' time—you'll look back and say, "Look where God has brought us from!" But don't stop there—keep on going. Before long, you'll realize that your house is half-paid for. Just keep walking, and a little bit later, you'll realize that you have so much money saved that if you draw it out, you can pay off your house and own it free and clear.

But you say, "It's not that simple!" Oh, yes, it is that simple! But you say, "Oh, we have medical bills!" Do you have faith? Start believing God for those medical bills to be paid off. And while you're at it, why not believe Him for your family to be healed?

Here's another news flash for you: You don't have to take expensive vacations. Use what you have wisely. Just take a vacation that lines up with what you have budgeted. If you can't afford it, don't take it. If you go ahead and take that expensive vacation, it will only be a curse to you...not a joy. During the whole time, you'll be sweating out how you're going to pay for that luxurious trip when you get back home. And what about the money for the gas you'll need to get back home? When you're out in the toolies and all you have in your pocket is $14.50 and you have five hundred miles left to cover, it's too late to pray one of those "faith prayers" for gas money to get back home. In times like those, you don't need more faith to get back home; YOU NEED WISDOM!

"But everybody is going to Europe! If we don't keep up, what will the neighbors think of us?" Who cares? Don't believe that lie! Take a vacation you can really enjoy—one you can afford to pay for. Half-steps.

Keep your witness before God, and He will bless your life. Just stay faithful along the way as you take that series of small half-steps. If you are going to serve God, it's very important that you learn to obey those small unctions He gives you along the way. Then when you hear the big unctions from God, you'll already know how to operate in them. Use wisdom.

Don't just blow it because you have it. Don't spend every dollar you have in your pocket. Put those dollars in the bank.

Faithfully taking these half-steps will cause you to advance spiritually to such a degree that one day you'll look around and realize with amazement that you are walking in biblical prosperity. God promised it, and His Word will not return to Him void.

4
Reasons Why God Wants Us to Prosper

Intellectually, we may know that God wants us to prosper; yet in our hearts, we wonder, *Does He really want everyone to prosper? Does that include me? And if so, then...why?* Sometimes knowing the "whys" helps us understand that it is indeed God's will for us to prosper.

Cindy and I have discovered over the years, that those "whys" are real important. We have three daughters who have asked us "why" on many occasions. "Why, Daddy? Why do we have to go to bed at nine o'clock?"

"So you'll grow up to be real strong and to look just like Mama," I may have replied. Or perhaps on another occasion the reply would be, "Because you need eight or nine hours of sleep at night in order to feel good tomorrow and have the energy you'll need to do your best."

"But *why?*"

"So your food will digest properly, and so you won't have a tummy ache during the night!"

"Why??"

"Because I said so! Now, go to bed!"

Anyone who has had experience parenting will relate to that answer! Why? Because anyone who has had experience parenting will probably have had to use that answer pretty frequently! Sometimes you just have to cut through all that other stuff...and get right to the point!

In reality, if we know the "whys" of something, it's a lot easier to accept the "what." I don't believe God ever requires us to believe anything without knowing why. The Word of God is filled with answers and reasons to believe God—and one of the things He clearly states is that He desires that we may prosper. If there was no other "why" except "God said it," that would be good enough for me.

God wants us to prosper, not perish

God wants us to prosper because He has work for us to do. There are those who need to hear about Jesus—and the only way they'll ever hear the Good News is if we tell them.

Yet many sincere, Holy Ghost-filled Christians are perishing instead of prospering in this hour. They are not on top. They're so busy keeping the wolf away from their door, they have little time to devote to the things of God and to the work He has assigned for them to do. Why is that? Let's look at 1 Corinthians 2:12, which states, *Now we have received, not the spirit of the world, but the spirit which is of God; that we might know the things that are freely given to us of God.* This passage of Scripture clearly states that by the Spirit of God, we can "know the things that are...given to us of God." In other words, by His Spirit, we can "know the things of God." But the Bible also says, *My people are destroyed for lack of knowledge* (Hosea 4:6). So it is possible to know the things of God...and to perish.

But if we perish, it is not for our lack of the Holy Ghost. We can have the Holy Spirit within us and still perish, because it is the lack of *knowledge* on our parts that causes this phenomenon. Conversely, studying the Bible to gain knowledge—and thereby, developing the mind of Christ within us—will cause us to prosper.

How do we come to know the things of God?

First, the Bible says we must seek God. *But seek ye first the kingdom of God, and his righteousness; and all these things shall be added unto you* (Matthew 6:33). Next, we must add faith: *Now faith is the substance of things hoped for, the evidence of things not seen* (Hebrews 11:1). Why? Because faith produces things. In fact, faith is the substance of all things. It is the evidence of things not seen. What do I mean by that? I mean that everything that begins in the mind of Christ, as His vision for our lives, is received by His Spirit into our spirits. Those things do not yet exist in the natural. But by faith, we get ahold of those things and begin to pray them forth, mixing our faith with God's promises and praying according to His Word. Eventually, if we don't back off, we'll see a manifestation in the natural of things that began as just a small vision from heaven. Now, some of those things may be material, but some are spiritual things. And one of those spiritual things is grace.

Let me translate that word *grace* for you: It means anything that comes from God. It means salvation. It means healing. It means restoration. It means love. Those things encompassed in the Word of God that pour down from Him can all be included in the definition of grace. Grace is the *charis*—or gift—of God, through Christ. That Greek word, *charis,* is the root word of *charisma,* which means "gifts of God." So it is important that we understand that this *charisma* of God plays an active role in the grace of God. We are saved by grace, but when we put that grace to work in our lives and the lives of others, then we see the operation of the *charisma*—gifts—of God. As the Holy Ghost gets to work, those of us who were saved by grace begin to do the work laid out for us, using the gifts of God within us. Thus, the gifts of the Holy Spirit are in operation within us in the course of our daily lives, and so we are called "charismatics."

We are the ones on earth who are actually doing the *charisma* of God. Yet there is more to grace than even salvation and the baptism in the Holy Spirit, and the resulting gifts imparted to us.

Grace is God's unmerited favor—the good things of God that are not dispersed to us according to our worthiness or unworthiness, our works or our accomplishments. God's grace is given freely. We receive it by faith—and faith really turns God on. Faith is the hand that reaches out to take the grace of God. Without faith, grace won't work. That is why God gave everyone a measure of faith. That measure of faith goes to work to obtain from God everything we need.

The gifts of the Spirit

The gifts of the Spirit, listed in chapter 12 of 1 Corinthians, are part of God's package of grace. I believe all Spirit-filled believers should operate in one or more of these spiritual gifts. But pastors, evangelists, and those called by God into full-time ministry should definitely move in more than one spiritual gift because, more than anyone else, they need them to accomplish the work at hand.

One gift a pastor should have is the gift of teaching. The Bible says a pastor must be able to teach (see Colossians 1:25-28). He must be able to speak and to teach under the inspiration of the Holy Spirit for the edification of his flock. I also believe a pastor should operate in the healing gifts. Now, that doesn't mean that everyone he lays his hands on will be healed. That is between the person in search of healing and God. But the pastor should be willing to boldly lay hands on the sick and pray for their recovery. He should also operate in the gift of discerning of spirits. There are enough deceptive wolves in sheeps' clothing out there to prove that's true! Devils will try to get into the church, unless the pastor has the gift of discerning of spirits in full operation. He must first learn how to deal with the spirits, then with the person and his problems.

First Corinthians, chapter 12, talks about another gift that I believe a pastor should operate in—and that's prophecy. I say if a pastor doesn't prophesy, he's missing step one of the gifts of the Spirit. He must not only edify, exhort, and comfort the flock—at times, he must boldly prophesy and proclaim, "Thus saith the Lord!"

I also believe a pastor should flow in the gifts of tongues and the interpretation of tongues. In my life and ministry, these gifts are frequently in operation.

God talks to us in two ways

First Corinthians 3:1 states: *And I, brethren, could not speak unto you as unto spiritual, but as unto carnal, even as unto babes in Christ.* Take a good look at that verse, because it reveals to us that God speaks to us in two ways—spiritual and carnal. He will either speak to our spirits, or He will speak to our heads. There is just one problem if God speaks to us in our heads; our heads are filled with all those other voices—the hurricanes and thunder and shazam of the slick advertising world...the way it affects our flesh...the attitudes and desires and opinions of others...and the way it affects our thinking. Yes, with all those things being funneled into us, it can be very hard to hear the voice of God. Yet when He speaks to our spirits, there is a directness about it that bypasses all those worldly influences.

But not everyone can hear God in his or her spirit at all times. That's why God speaks to you in two ways—either to your head...or to your heart.

In order to hear God speak to your spirit-man, you need to learn to tune in your spirit-man so that when He speaks, it registers in your spirit...not just in your head.

Meat, not milk

The church at Corinth had a few problems in its day. The people of Corinth were still very carnal in the sense that they had not developed themselves spiritually to hear the voice of God. Hebrews 5:14 states, *But strong meat belongeth to them that are of full age, even those who by reason of use have their senses exercised to discern both good and evil.* In this verse, we are given a good lesson on how to hear God. We are told that we must exercise our senses to discern between good and evil...right and wrong...the things of God and the things of the devil. The person who is mature is the one who has developed the ability to discern these things.

The presence of the gifts of the Spirit in someone's life is not necessarily a sign of that individual's spiritual maturity or level of spiritual development. A person can be born again, filled with the Holy Spirit, and receive supernatural gifts—yet be very immature and undeveloped spiritually. Perhaps a person's lack is in the area of character—or in the carnal nature that has yet to be developed through studying the Word of God...or perhaps it is some lack in their relationship to God—

yet this person may still have some very powerful spiritual gifts in operation. This indicates that the presence of the gifts of the Holy Spirit are not necessarily a sign of a person's level of spirituality.

God said the sign of true spiritual maturity is the ability to discern between good and evil. To develop this ability, you must allow the unction of the Holy Ghost to develop in you. You must allow the Holy Ghost to teach you how to discern.

I am constantly amazed at the number of tongue-talking Christians who absolutely cannot—or will not—discern between good and evil. Consequently, they go to movies that contain all sorts of filthy things—including murder, blood, and violence—when one of the Ten Commandments clearly states, "Don't murder." To some people, their idea of entertainment is watching characters in a blood-and-guts movie murder one another! But after filling their minds with such evil, it's no wonder they can't hear the voice of God in their spirits!

Yet they may say, "Well, at least there wasn't any *sex* in that movie—just a lot of blood!" But I say, "Didn't the same Jesus who said, 'Don't commit adultery,' also say, 'Don't commit murder'?"

People who are constantly feeding on a diet of this visual junk must sit there and take it in, overriding their consciences. Then they wonder why God can't talk to them in their spirits. Why? Because it won't register. There's too much buildup. If these same people would just learn to discern between good and evil and become sensitive to the leading of the Holy Spirit, they would stop doing what is displeasing to the Lord...and find that they were becoming sensitive to His voice, so that when He spoke, it would register immediately in their spirits.

Choose the right spiritual diet

First Corinthians 3:2 clearly indicates that there are two ways to be fed from God's Word: *I have fed you with milk, and not with meat: for hitherto ye were not able to bear it, neither yet now are ye able.* As Christians, we want to make certain that we are feeding on the meat of the Word...not simply existing on a spiritual diet of milk only. However, the only thing that will keep us on milk is our inability to receive meat!

Verse 3: *For ye are yet carnal: for whereas there is among you envying, and strife, and divisions, are ye not carnal, and walk as men?* James 3:16 reinforces that passage, admonishing, *For where envying and strife is, there is confusion and every evil work.* Just think about that for a moment! James said envying and strife open the door to every definition of evil you can imagine. Every demonic work will be able to come into your life, simply because envy and strife are present. They are doorways to the devil, and they include anger, jealousy, and bitterness.

The passage in 1 Corinthians continues: *For while one saith, I am of Paul; and another, I am of Apollos; are ye not carnal? Who then is Paul, and who is Apollos, but ministers by whom ye believed...?* (3:4,5). Now, let that sink in for a moment. Who were the apostles? Men—the same as any minister alive today. No preacher is divine! You belong to Jesus Christ. He is the Great Shepherd. Each pastor is simply an undershepherd of the Great Shepherd.

Let me repeat—no one owns you except Jesus Christ. He bought you with His blood, and no one else on this planet can tell you what to do...except Him. Only Jesus may tell you what to do...and even then, whether or not you accept or reject it is between just you and Him. Make sure He's number one in your life...and that serving Him is your number-one priority.

Verse 6: *I have planted, Apollos watered; but God gave the increase.* Again we see the principle of sowing and reaping...and of increase. *God gave the increase.* Many of you already have testimonies about how God has increased you. But I've got good news for you: God isn't through with you yet! He's going to bless you some more. Why? Because He is a God of increase, and it is His good pleasure to increase you. In fact, He's going to increase you even more, as you continue on that upward path toward Him. Stay on it; it is not the will of the Father for you to take two steps forward...only to take one step back. He wants you to keep moving from glory to glory

...faith to faith...victory to victory...triumph to triumph ...mountaintop to mountaintop.

God said His people would be *the head, and not the tail* (Deuteronomy 28:13). He is raising up His Church to be the head, and not the tail. He wants His people to be blessed in the city and blessed in the field, blessed going out and blessed coming in. Yet so many Christians have a poverty mentality when it comes to God. They do not comprehend that God wants to bless them—that He can, in fact, place them in the midst of the largest city in the world or in the world's biggest jungle, and bless them right where they are. He says He will bless His people, and He always performs His Word.

James 4:13 says, *Go to now, ye that say, To day or to morrow we will go into such a city, and continue there a year, and buy and sell, and get gain.* As God revealed to James, He wants His people to make a profit; He wants them to buy and sell and profit from the process. But God's program of blessing involves more than simple buying and selling and profit-making; it involves using those profits in the correct way, according to heaven's economy.

God does not simply desire that people get rich and sock away a lot of money in the bank. Those who are doing that are in sin, and their money will testify against them in judgment one day. Those who are doing that are not using their money the way God would have them use it. But thank God for those who are giving of what they have according to the Word of God— those who retain nine-tenths of what they make for themselves but give the first tenth to God. The Bible says their alms will always come before God as a memorial (see Acts 10:4).

James continues, in verses 14 and 15: *Whereas ye know not what shall be on the morrow. For what is your life? It is even a vapour, that appeareth for a little time, and then vanisheth away. For that ye ought to say, If the Lord will....* From these verses, we see that even the best plans are subject to the will of God. We think our various plans will work out in a certain way, yet whether or not tomorrow even comes is forever subject to the will of God.

For the person whose whole life is wrapped up in his bank account, it is difficult to understand that God does indeed desire that he prosper—but for a different reason than simply getting richer by the day as the interest mounts up. There is a reason for God wanting that person to prosper.

But now ye rejoice in your boastings: all such rejoicing is evil. Therefore to him that knoweth to do good, and doeth it not, to him it is sin. Go to now, ye rich men, weep and howl for your miseries that shall come upon you. Your riches are corrupted, and your garments are motheaten. Your gold and silver is cankered; and the rust of them shall be a witness against you... (James 4:16-5:3).

As I was reading these verses one day, the Holy Ghost said to me, "There are many whom God has blessed who will stand before Me on judgment day with their bank accounts full of rust because they have not used their money wisely. Their bank accounts will testify against their own words."

You see, God wants you to be blessed FOR TWO REASONS: so the gospel of Jesus will go throughout the earth, and so you can have seed to sow and bread to eat. The Lord does not desire that we merely build storehouses to stash our money in, then kick back and live the high life. Jesus said, "Your soul will be required of you if you have that mentality toward money" (see Luke 12:19,20).

God wants you to prosper. He wants you to pay every bill. He knows there is bread required and seed that needs to be sown. As I've reminded God many times, it takes more bread in the nineties than it did in the eighties. He wants that car note paid. He wants that electric bill paid. He wants the college expenses of your children to be paid. He wants you to have food to eat, and He wants your children to be properly clothed. He knows what you need; ask Him! He'll give it to you, but He also requires that you be faithful with what He gives to you!

The Word says there are those who have *heaped treasure together for the last days* (James 5:3). This is contrary to God's mandate for us in this hour. We're claiming the blood of Jesus for these last days—that is our door, our key to entering into this new move of God on earth. The blood of Jesus. When you and I stand before the Lord on judgment day, we want to be covered in the blood and able to stand there clothed in the righteousness of Christ.

In the parable of the marriage supper, we see that there were those who were properly clothed in wedding garments... and those who were not. Those who were improperly attired were cast into outer darkness where there was weeping and gnashing of teeth (see Matthew 22:11-13). When God calls the roll for the marriage supper of the Lamb, we must be properly attired. We won't be able to pull out our checkbooks on that day and write out a big check to cover the deficit. We must be paid up in advance, clothed in righteousness, and covered in the blood.

Yet many today place their confidence in money. This is quite ironic, since money is continually being devalued in today's shifting global economy. Salvation is the only thing that will defeat the curse of death—money won't do it.

Behold, the hire of the labourers who have reaped down your fields, which is of you kept back by fraud, crieth: and the cries of them which have reaped are entered into the ears of the Lord of sabaoth (James 5:4). When I read that verse, I am convinced that the Lord was speaking not of someone who pays low wages but about Jesus. Jesus looked out upon the harvest fields and saw that they were white—ready to harvest. The fields, of course, were symbolic of souls waiting to be saved. So Jesus said to His disciples, *Pray ye therefore the Lord of the harvest, that he will send forth labourers into his harvest...* (Matthew 9:38). Every preacher who stands up and says, "I need money to help take the gospel of Jesus Christ to the world" is one of those laborers whose cries come before God each day. And at times, their work is hindered by those who withhold from God. That, I believe, is what this passage of Scripture means. When people withhold from God, they are holding back by fraud that which would help one of these laborers take the gospel into places like Managua, Nicaragua...Aroyo, Honduras...Dublin, Ireland.

For one million dollars, it is possible to reach a million souls by satellite. That's a dollar apiece. I don't believe that in the three years of Jesus' earthly ministry, He preached to a million people. Yet He said, "Greater works than these shall ye do...." In this life, we will probably never meet the majority of souls won through this ministry. And of those who accept Christ through our television broadcasts, many will never send us a penny—and that is not what is important to us. But there will be a reward for us because we preached the gospel. And if you helped pay for the air time during which we preached, you'll share in the same reward.

We plan to preach the gospel to the entire world—and that takes money. God knows it takes money, and He will multiply what we have, as long as we continue to use wisely that which He has entrusted to us. *Be patient therefore, brethren, unto the coming of the Lord. Behold, the husbandman waiteth for the precious fruit of the earth...* (James 5:7). What is that precious fruit? Souls!

Jesus was the original Seed. The Bible says, in First Corinthians, that He was planted into the earth. When He died, He went into the earth, was covered up as the stone was rolled over the opening of His tomb...and on the third day, He arose...firstborn of the dead. He is Lord of the harvest, Lord of the increase. He is the Vine, and He has been gathering a harvest of precious fruit from that Vine ever since!

The God of increase

God gives the increase. This may or may not be in relation to money, but it does include finances. I get excited about the fact that God gives increase. I circle scriptures like 1 Corinthians 3:7: *...neither is he that planteth any thing, neither he that watereth; but God that giveth the increase.* I highlight these verses real good because when I study these scriptures, I can clearly see that God is a giver. He loves to give to His people. He loved the world so much that He gave His only Son (see John 3:16). Romans 8:32 tells us just how generous God is: *He that spared not his own Son, but delivered him up for us all,* *how shall he not with him also freely give us all things?* And Matthew 6:33 states, *But seek ye first the kingdom of God, and his righteousness; and all these things shall be added—* given...increased—*unto you.* From these verses, we can see that God is a giver and that, in fact, He does not wish to take anything away from us...except fear, sickness, and poverty.

First Corinthians 3:8,9 says, *Now he that planteth and he that watereth are one: and every man shall receive his own reward according to his own labour. For we are labourers together with God....* Now, this is where it really gets good! This passage of Scripture says we are co-laborers with God! One day I spent some time just thinking about that concept. As I was meditating on it, the Holy Ghost began to speak to me. He said, "We are laborers together with God." Now, I believe God is the bigger part of that tandem. I believe He's the larger part of our ministry of togetherness. He's the Big Brother, and I am His child—His little brother.

Jesus labored alone

Then I began to think about Jesus and how He came to earth...alone. He was born of a virgin. Man had nothing to do with His conception and birth. God did it all. He is the One who conceived Jesus in the womb of Mary. Man did not create Jesus; He was God in the flesh. It is yet a great mystery—God with us...Emmanuel.

When Jesus walked on earth, He ministered for three-and-a-half years, revealing again and again, through miracle after miracle, that He was God with us—the Messiah. Yet there weren't a handful of people who followed Him. And when He died, He died alone—all by himself—an excruciatingly painful death upon a Roman cross. None of that handful of disciples ran up and offered to take the punishment in His stead. None said, "Jesus, I'll take Your place!" Jesus died alone. Humiliated. A borrowed grave awaited His crucified body. His friends forsook Him, just as the Prophet Isaiah had written: *...we did esteem him stricken, smitten of God...* (Isaiah 53:4).

When Jesus breathed His last breath, the skies split and darkness descended, even though it was daytime. Then Jesus descended into hell. What He did there, He did by himself. He defeated the devil. Michael, the archangel, didn't have to help Him. A company of warring angels did not descend into hell with Him. When Jesus arose from the grave, He brought redeemed souls with Him. He purchased their souls—and yours and mine—with His blood. And He did it all by himself.

So Jesus' earthly ministry was a labor of loneliness. He was despised, rejected, and He labored alone. You may say, "That's the kind of ministry I want." But I say, "Oh, no, that's not what God said. He said you would be a co-laborer with Him." Why? Because when Jesus went to the Father, He sent another Comforter—the Holy Spirit—and He will live in you.

Jesus sent the Comforter so we could stop laboring alone on earth and start co-laboring with Him. He said, "We're co-laborers together. The works that I do, you will do...and even greater works...because I'll be in you and we'll work together."

Just think for a moment what it means to be co-laborers with Christ, and you can't help but see something pretty powerful. The Holy Ghost, who is the Person of God on earth today, lives within you. He is in constant communication with God and Jesus, who is as much God as the Father. The Three are One. Thus, when you are a co-laborer with Christ, you are a co-laborer with the Trinity. The Three are One. There is no division. There is no distinction.

What it means to co-labor with God

When you lay hands on the sick, it is the Holy Ghost in you who is laying hands on the sick. When you cast out devils, it is the Holy Ghost in you who is casting out devils. When you enter the ministry, it is the Holy Ghost in you who is entering the ministry right along with you. You are, after all, co-laborers.

When you tithe and give offerings, the Holy Ghost is right there with you, tithing and giving. Co-laboring. And if you sit down on your "blessed assurance" and don't do anything, the Holy Ghost has to sit down right along with you; there is nothing He can do without you co-laboring. Nothing will take place. If you don't co-labor, He can't co-labor. If you don't give, He can't give. If you don't preach, He can't preach. It takes two.

Believe me, if you don't allow God to raise you up so that He can co-labor with you, He will raise someone else up to do the job. And if everyone else also decides to sit down and do nothing, He'll raise up a donkey or a rock to do the job. I don't know about you, but I'm not going to let a donkey or a rock steal my crown!

God wants to magnify the ministry of Jesus

Through the work of the Holy Spirit on earth, God wants to magnify the ministry of Jesus. To do that, He needs you and me. I know that God wants to vindicate the work of Calvary in the earth. After all, the Word of God clearly states that it is not God's will *that any should perish, but that all should come to repentance* (2 Peter 3:9). But just because God wants something to take place does not necessarily mean that it *will*.

You see, people have a choice.

Before I was a pastor, I operated a business. I know from experience that there are different types of workers. When you find an employer who is a good, hard worker, you actually feel like you are co-laboring with that person. The good worker doesn't run around carrying tales and running down the company. They'll do just the opposite. They'll speak well of you. They'll tell you, "I'm so glad I have this job! I work for a good boss. I'm so glad this company is here and stable and not about to fold." This is the sort of worker you can count on to help pull you through the bad times. And if you were considering giving out promotions, this is the sort of person you'd consider first to receive one.

It's the same with the kingdom of God. Just as in running a business, it would be foolish not to promote the person with the right attitude—so it is in God's kingdom. Just as you would give an increase to the person who is maintaining the right relationship to you and your business, so it is in God's kingdom. Those who speak well of the house of God and who are rightly related to Him—they are the ones who are first in line for promotion in God's kingdom. These individuals will increase. God will bless them.

Conversely, God will not give increase to those who will not co-labor with Him in the earth today. If they talk bad behind peoples' backs, if they run down the church, if they run down different ministries, God will say, "Don't give increase to this person—just give increases to those who are co-laborers with Me."

This idea of across-the-board pay increases can't be found in God's kingdom. That's an idea promoted by the unions, but it's not God's system.

A heart for souls

As I will elaborate on later in this book, the heartbeat of God is souls. To be a co-laborer with Him means to win souls—to get people saved. God's primary goal on earth today is to get people inside His ark of safety—inside the kingdom of heaven—not just to maintain our own little lives. To co-labor with God is a whole lot bigger than just taking care of our own households.

Now, if the Rapture takes place in my lifetime, that's great: It means I'm out of here on the first load...I'm going to heaven on the Big Ride! But if it doesn't, I'll still say, "Glory to God! I get to work a little longer for Jesus!"

Cindy and I made a decision many years ago to do whatever we could to preach to every single household in the Gulf Coast region of Texas, and then to take the gospel to every corner of the world. For eight-and-a-half years we labored to do that in the manner God taught us—the manner that works. That is the manner I am relating to you in the pages of this book. It seemed that we were making steady progress...and then the Holy Ghost began to change things. Everything seemed to be moving forward quickly—with light-speed compared to the many years we had spent steadily plodding ahead.

That's when the Holy Ghost began to speak so powerfully to me about the years immediately ahead—between now and the year 2000. He said, "In twenty-four months, you won't recognize your ministry at Abundant Life Christian Center, it will have changed so much."

Nobody likes change much. It's not comfortable. But think about it. Think where you were two years ago...and where you are now. What is the common denominator? Change. It's going to happen whether or not you like it. But when God is involved in the change, you're going to like it.

The Holy Ghost told me, "You and I are going after souls, and I'll break with the traditional ways of doing that." Well, that was good news to me because I just want to get people into the kingdom of God...lots of people.

You may say, "Well, it sounds like all you're after is numbers!"

And I'll say, "You bet. It's not just numbers I'm after...it's numbers, in Jesus' name. Let's take what we have to the masses, in Jesus' name. Thank God, we have something the world needs to hear."

So doors began to open for us on television—on TBN, on the late Lester Sumrall's satellite ministry, and on BET. We took the good news of the gospel to the airwaves, and as God gave us the increase, we began to participate in seeing many more souls won for Christ than ever before in our ministry. Why? Because God gave the increase, just as He promised to do in His Word.

The Lord desires that His people prosper so they can lead. The Word says His people will be the head and not the tail. He has leadership lined up for His people, but in order to lead, we're going to have to lose that "poverty mentality."

Unfortunately, many Christians have that poverty mentality when it comes to God, but that has to go. We're going to have to come to the understanding that God wants to bless us. He wants to bless us in the city. He wants to bless us in the field. He wants to bless us in the jungles...and in the highways and byways.

How do we know that God wants us to prosper? Because His Word says so (see 1 John 1:2). And that's good enough for me!

5
Spiritual Answers to Spiritual Problems

It's not enough just to know the words of God. You can have the words of God mixed with the ways of the world and still have nothing to show for it. As Spirit-filled Christians, we want the *words of God* mixed with the *power of the Holy Ghost*—because when that happens we get something called the *ways of God.*

Thirty-five years ago the Holy Ghost opened up a new way of ministry. There was a group of men—including Oral Roberts—who began to take the gospel to the television and radio airwaves. They preached all over the world and revolutionized the way the gospel was seen and heard on earth. Previously, the preaching of the Word had been limited to large arenas and specially-built tents that would seat large numbers of people. With the advent of television, more people than ever before in history could hear the Word go forth in a single sermon.

Great ministries were raised up to take the Word to the uttermost parts of the earth in this new era of high-tech communication. Oral Roberts, for instance, is the only man of this generation to build a Bible school, a major university, a seminary, a law school, and a medical school. The only other person to ever do that was Johns Hopkins—but Johns Hopkins didn't preach to a hundred million people a year, as did Oral Roberts.

Now, I'm not saying, "Praise the name of Oral." What I am saying is that Oral Roberts' accomplishments for the kingdom of God have been unprecedented...exceptional.

Intellectualism as spirituality

God's ways are higher than our ways. That's what God reminded me of one day, as He spoke to me. He said, "Intellectualism is not mentality. Intellectualism is spirituality. Intellectualism affects people very powerfully. Anytime you start breaking into a higher train of thought...rationality...reasoning, that mode of thinking becomes very captivating." The Holy Ghost revealed to me that while often very gratifying, very motivating—even very visionary—intellectualism can also become very distracting. "That is because intellectualism is not only mental—it's spiritual," the Holy Ghost said.

Now, when God shows you something that's quite visionary, you can either give it up to God and allow Him to use it His way, or keep it for yourself and become captivated by it, as is often the case with intellectualism. Intellectualism can quickly lead to humanism, and what is humanism but man's desire to create God in his own (man's) image?

A new kind of preaching

So when God began to raise up this group of men to minister thirty-five years ago, they ministered in an entirely new way. They did not speak to man's intellect. They spoke to man's spirit. These were men who could see on another level, preach on another level—on the level of the Word. Rather than turning their own natural talents and abilities into money-making endeavors in the business world, and rather than becoming pompous and prideful, these men were used mightily by God to advance His kingdom on earth. They accomplished great things.

In addition to Oral Roberts, there was Rex Humbard. Brother Rex and his wife, Maude Aimee, began to preach the gospel on TV in a day when this was unprecedented. They have since preached to countless millions and won large numbers of men, women, and children to the Lord.

Pat Robertson had just seventy dollars in his pocket when the Lord told him to move his wife and kids from New York to some "podunk" place in Virginia and buy a TV station. The

Lord wanted Pat Robertson to take back the airwaves from the prince of the power of the air—Satan. Pat Robertson acted in obedience to God, and that was the beginning of "The 700 Club" and CBN. The rest is history.

Paul and Jan Crouch caught the vision for a global Christian television network from the Holy Ghost, who said He would "use the foolish things of this world to confound the wise." Because they were obedient to God and followed His direction to accomplish something they had no idea how to accomplish in their own might, they were raised up to take Christian television programming to a new level—then take it all over the world.

There's a man in Tulsa, Oklahoma, by the name of Kenneth Hagin. The Lord spoke to him about starting a Bible school. When he began to make his plans to start such a school, he was an itinerate Assembly of God evangelist who rarely drew crowds larger than 150 people. But the Holy Ghost kept speaking to him about starting a Bible school, and soon he began to see it in his spirit. He caught the vision, and it came to pass. He founded Rhema Bible School in Broken Arrow, Oklahoma, just outside Tulsa, and thousands of Rhema graduates have taken Brother Hagin's Word of Faith teaching around the world.

Each of these men is quite intellectual in his own right. You could sit down and have a conversation with any one of these men and be blown away at their intellectual ability. The point I'm making is that each of these men determined not to operate in their own intelligence, their own financial ability, their own talent, their own creativity. They started out by taking what little they had and giving it to God, as did the young boy who offered up his lunch to Jesus so the five thousand could be fed. God took what they had and multiplied it many times over. And He's still doing it on earth today.

God wants our minds to prosper too

God is a giver. That means He wants every aspect of our being to prosper. That means our minds, our wills, our emotions. That means our spirits, our souls, our bodies. Yes, that even means that God wants our minds to prosper.

Now, some Holy Ghost-filled people get real nervous when you start talking about the mind. Some believe you shouldn't even address that mental realm—but stick to the spiritual realm. I maintain that if you and I don't address the mind and find out what the Word of God says about it, then the devil certainly will! He'll teach people all about the mind and its various wonders. But God does not condemn thinking, reasoning, the intellect. Why would He even give us those things if He didn't want us to use them?

Every person has the capacity to think and to reason. Those functions of the mind date back to the Garden of Eden, when Adam and Eve used reasoning to set their will to eat the forbidden fruit. It was their reasoning capacity that the devil went to work on in planting seeds of doubt about God's word to them regarding the outcome of eating from the forbidden tree. The devil told Adam and Eve that to eat the fruit would make them "like God."

Who wouldn't want to be a little smarter than they are at one time or another? After all, scientists have concluded that even the smartest person alive only uses about one to three percent of his brain. Does this mean that when we receive our glorified bodies in heaven, we'll also have brains that function at 100-percent capacity? That's something to think about.

Adam, prior to the fall, must have had a fully functioning mental capacity. After all, he named every animal in God's creation, tended the garden single-handedly, and walked and talked with God face-to-face daily. Yet the smarter people get, the less they tend to believe the simplicity of the story of creation as portrayed in the Book of Genesis.

Those who discount God must rely entirely on that which they can comprehend in the mental realm. If medicine can't cure them, they'll die. And often medicine is not able to bring about a cure. People are living shorter lives because of their little bit of knowledge and their trust in medical science instead of the things of God. That spirit of the world has captivated them and blinded them to the simplicity of believing God for what they need.

But when a person gives his or her life to Jesus, something happens. They are born again. The spirit of the world leaves them, and a great exchange takes place. The Spirit of God fills them. No wonder their emotions begin to change! No wonder their health improves! No wonder their thinking patterns begin to change as they begin to motivate that wonderful thing called the mind with the life-producing Word of God!

In Ephesians 4:23, we are told to renew our minds in the Word of God. That's our insurance in the war going on against our minds, waged anew each day by the devil and his minions.

So how do we prevail against this warfare? The Holy Ghost teaches us how. In 1 Corinthians 2:13, we read, *Which things also we speak, not in the words which man's wisdom teacheth, but which the Holy Ghost teacheth; comparing spiritual things with spiritual.* Another translation says, "Comparing spiritual things of the Old Covenant with the spiritual things of the New Covenant." So by the revelation of the Holy Ghost, we have spiritual revelation. And we need that because as Christians, there will be many spiritual things presented to us. But not all of these things are good for us. So we must discern which things to pay heed to and which things to reject. We need not rely on man's teaching. We can pray until we receive a spiritual answer from the Holy Ghost.

The Bible says Christians should be able to discern the difference between what is of God and what is not of God. If something is not of God, we will have an inner witness to that effect. There will be an immediate quickening. My rule of thumb is—if I'm not sure, then the answer is "no."

We can keep our spiritual edge by staying in the Word, so that when that quickening comes—when something just doesn't set right—we can find a basis in the Word for whether or not to receive it.

If you will just obey God, it's amazing what He can do for you. You will learn to operate in the timing of the Lord, doing the will of the Lord. To be led by God is often contrary to intellectualism. In fact, it may seem quite foolish at times.

Intellectualism must be used correctly

I am not saying that a person should not be intelligent or operate in the intellectual realm. I am saying, however, that a person should not use that intellectualism for purposes other than serving God—because intellectualism alone will make a person miserable. What was intended to be a blessing can instead become a curse. It can fill a person with questions for which there are no hard-and-fast answers, short of hearing from God. Furthermore, it can slam shut the door of heaven. Many men and women who had the potential of greatness for God within them turned and went the other way when confronted with the rational views supported by intellectualism. God is always reminding us that His ways—and His thoughts—are higher than ours. And in that light, there can be no such thing as a true intellectual.

During the days of Elijah, there lived a man in the same region of the world called Mohammed. Faced with biblical truths, and also a visionary, Mohammed elected to reject God's ways. God's ways just didn't seem to line up with his own intellectual views, so he founded his own religion—Islam. He developed himself into the prophet Mohammed, and Moslems all over the world continue to venerate him and follow his teachings in the pages of the Koran.

The Holy Ghost has shown me that a person should never try to develop himself, but should take "self" and offer it up before God in prayer for Him to develop along the lines of His perfect plan.

God wants to use each one of us. For each of us, there is a perfect plan. God wants to use each of us as His vessel. Since we have just one life to live, we need God's direction if we are to become all we were intended to be in this one lifetime. How will we ever achieve all we were intended to achieve for Him if we don't yield ourselves to Him?

There are countless instances of people whose lives could have been used mightily for God, but they turned and went their own way. There are others who begin to serve God and achieve a measure of success. Then they stop, turn around, and begin to follow their own agendas.

God wants all of us—all the time. He wants our hearts ...our hands...our feet...our mouths—not just as we begin our walks with Him, but always. He wants all of us, beginning to end. That's His plan. We should never forget where God has brought us from, but we should also never lose sight of where He's leading us. Thank God, our ultimate destination is heaven. But in the meantime, there is work for us to do—right here, right now, on earth.

Compassion for the multitudes

But when he saw the multitudes, he was moved with compassion on them, because they fainted, and were scattered abroad, as sheep having no shepherd. Then saith he unto his disciples, The harvest truly is plenteous, but the labourers are few; Pray ye therefore the Lord of the harvest, that he will send forth labourers into his harvest (Matthew 9:36-38).

And Jesus went forth, and saw a great multitude, and was moved with compassion toward them, and he healed their sick. And when it was evening, his disciples came to him, saying, This a desert place, and the time is now past; send the multitude away, that they may go into the villages, and buy themselves victuals. But Jesus said unto them, They need not depart; give ye them to eat. And they say unto him, We have here but five loaves, and two fishes. He said, Bring them hither to me.
—Matthew 14:14-18

The day Jesus fed the multitude on the side of a hill, the Bible says He looked out on them, gathered there—filled with so many needs—*and was moved with compassion toward them.* That's how *we* should be.

We need spiritual eyes to see people as they really are, and eyes of compassion to see their needs correctly. Jesus did not simply look out upon a sea of nameless faces. He looked out and saw thousands of individuals, each of whom had needs. Hunger was just one of their needs, but before He could fill those other needs, first He had to take care of the most immediate need—food.

The Bible says Jesus *saw* the multitude. He didn't just look into one face and stop there. He saw the big picture. He saw all of their problems. And if we are to move in the destiny of God in this hour, we must do the same. This world of ours is filled with great problems. The Church must not take the attitude of washing our hands of sinners and thinking, "You bunch of sinners, you're just getting what you deserve!"

Our attitude must match that of Jesus. He would not have looked at the homosexual community with anything less than compassion. Jesus may not approve of homosexuality, but He loves homosexuals. He has compassion upon them, and He can set them free. He has the same compassion for drug addicts, alcoholics, prostitutes, thieves, liars, and murderers. He does not approve of the sins, but He loves all sinners equally—and He can set them free.

The multitude gathered on the side of the hill before Jesus that day needed signs and wonders. Why? They had no food. When Jesus looked out upon the multitude, He saw sins like adultery and homosexuality, addiction, greed, murder, lying, cheating—and more. He didn't say, "You miserable sinners—you're messed up because you're reaping what you've sown!" No, He had mercy upon them, and regardless of their current spiritual state, He began to make arrangements for everyone present to be fed.

But the only food made available that day to feed the massive crowd consisted of five loaves and two fishes. Anyone could see that those modest provisions would barely feed two people, much less thousands. Nevertheless, Jesus took what He had been given, and lifted the loaves and fishes toward heaven and blessed them. And then the miracles began.

Why miracles?

We need miracles on earth today. This is an evil time we're living in. According to many signs contained in the Bible, we are undoubtedly living in the last days, and there will come many more perilous times.

Strange diseases are running rampant throughout the earth in these last days. AIDS is just one of them. Now there is a strain of strep virus that is literally "flesh-eating" in nature. Doctors say this virus can eat as much as an inch of human flesh per hour. Short of the mercy of God, we humans don't have a chance against these raging, hard-to-treat diseases that are part of the apocalyptic package unleashed on this planet during this hour.

So it seems quite obvious to me that we need signs, wonders, and miracles—daily—just to make it!

Thank God, there are Spirit-filled, Holy Ghost-filled, tongue-talking people on earth today who believe in casting out demons, laying on hands, releasing their faith, operating in the gifts of the Spirit, and witnessing the corresponding manifestation of signs and wonders on earth today.

I'm not a politician, so I can't offer political answers. I'm not a financier, so I can't offer financial answers. But I am blood-bought, Spirit-filled, and called by God to preach His Word. So, by His grace and under the inspiration of the Holy Ghost, I can offer some divine answers, as given to me by God—and we need that in this hour. Politics and financial institutions will run out of ideas and solutions—but God will always have an answer. He will always have the last word on earth.

Thank God that when we have a need, we can go to God—who has all the answers...all the time. When we need healing from some strange virus that doesn't even have a name yet, much less a man-made cure, we can go to God for our healing.

Thank God that when we need financial blessing, and the bank won't return our phone calls, we can go to Him for financial blessings.

The world's system will one day come to the end of its rope, but God never will. Medicine is not the answer, and money is not the answer. God is the answer. He is the solution.

The Word says that when Jesus looked out upon the multitude, He was filled with compassion. But He didn't stop there because the people didn't need compassion alone—they needed food. So Jesus, performing a miracle of great proportion that day, took a small ration of bread and fish and fed many thousands with it.

People are the same today. They don't simply need compassion—they need actual help. They need real solutions to their very real problems—problems that are overwhelming, insurmountable with anything less than a miracle because in the natural, there is just no hope.

Spiritual problems...spiritual answers

Problems always have a spiritual source, and so do the solutions to those problems. The solution is spiritual. His name is Jesus.

When the gospel of the kingdom is preached and faith enters the heart of a man or woman, the Holy Ghost begins to work. Then the angels of God join in as faith begins to build, and miracles start to germinate. The gifts of the Spirit begin to operate. Revelation knowledge begins to work, revealing the spiritual source. Finally, the Spirit of God pinpoints the problem and sends the correct solution.

Somebody once said, "You can give a man a fish and he'll be hungry tomorrow, but if you teach a man to fish, he'll never go hungry again." It's the same with spiritual things. The world is full of problems. If you give a man a "quick fix," he'll be back again tomorrow—hungry and full of need. But share Jesus—the Source of all answers—and man need never go hungry again.

One day the Holy Ghost spoke to my heart and said, "I'm going to send you people with problems." I thought, *Now, why are You telling me this? Every pastor I know of has his share of people with problems!* But the Lord said, "No—I am sending you sick people, people in debt, people who have been through divorces and all kinds of family problems. I am going to send you people who have been in every kind of church fight in this region."

So I said, "I quit!" No, not really! I called our elders and deacons together and told them what God had just spoken to my spirit. "God told me He was going to send us people with problems," I said. "But He told me, 'Never be a party to their problems—always be a part of the solution.'"

In order to do that, I learned to model myself after Jesus, who had compassion on the multitude, then did something about it. He sent the solution.

When people with problems come to me for help, they shouldn't expect me to get down there on the same level with that problem and commiserate with them in it. But they should expect me to give them what God's Word says about the solution to that problem. I would assume that in telling me about the problem, this person is looking for a way out—deliverance. They want to break free.

What I have discovered is that every problem has a spiritual root...and a spiritual answer. That spiritual answer comes when the Word of God is mixed with the Holy Ghost, by faith.

Money can't buy spiritual answers!

When someone lies gravely ill in the hospital, a person will do no good, showing up with a million dollars or showering that sick person with diamonds and rubies. The cure, in most cases, isn't for sale. You could cover a person from head to toe with gold dust and do no good whatsoever. But if you come to them in the name of the Lord, speaking the Word, laying hands on this sick person, they will get well. That sickness will have to go. That person will have the opportunity to be made whole in that hour—and that wholeness will have been offered to them free of charge, in the name of Jesus.

So those of us who come in that Name, come with answers. We don't just show up to listen to a bunch of problems. Anyone can do that. We come in the name of the Lord, with answers from His Word. And that is what the world needs in this hour.

This world is so fragmented that it really has nothing to offer–except shattered lives. The best the world can offer is to break your heart, break up your home, steal your children, siphon away your finances, and fragment everything you have. But those of us who know God and serve Him, come with answers. We don't come just to "pet" problems, or even to teach people how to deal with them. We come with the ultimate answer to these great problems that plague mankind.

So the hurting people who are flocking into the house of God in this hour, when problems have never been so great on earth, are coming to the right place. They don't come merely expecting compassion—although we certainly are moved with compassion—but they come expecting to receive answers from the Word of God.

One Body, bound by love

We are, after all, woven together by the thread of love to create the body of Christ. If one member hurts, then the entire Body suffers. The love of God that never fails is what unites us together as one Body. Jesus was moved to compassion as He looked out upon the multitude gathered on the hillside the day He performed the miracle of the multiplied loaves and fishes. Why was He so moved? The Bible says He was moved because He saw that the people had no shepherd.

The word *shepherd* is another term for "pastor." A pastor is patterned after the shepherd of biblical times, who led his flock through rocky places. When the going got tough and some of the sheep began to stray, the shepherd took the appropriate means—either by using a crooked staff or perhaps a dog—to bring the wayward sheep back into the flock once more. Now, goats require a different kind of herdsman. Goats are obstinate and must be driven—not led. But sheep are meek animals and can be led.

Jesus is our Shepherd. He saw mankind as sheep without a shepherd, and it moved Him to compassion. Do you realize that every person on this planet has the potential of becoming one of Jesus' sheep? I believe the greatest evangelists of all time will be raised up in this final hour before the Rapture to preach to every sheep who will hear the Word of God. And those who obey that word can enter into the fold of Christ.

The fields are white unto harvest. It's time.

Lessons from the woman at the well

There cometh a woman of Samaria to draw water [from the well of Jacob]: *Jesus saith unto her, Give me to drink....Then saith the woman of Samaria unto him, How is it that thou, being a Jew, askest drink of me, which am a woman of Samaria? for the Jews have no dealings with the Samaritans. Jesus answered and said unto her, If thou knewest the gift of God, and who it is that saith to thee, Give me to drink; thou wouldest have asked of him, and he would have given thee living water....Whosoever drinketh of this water shall thirst again: But whosoever drinketh of the water that I shall give him shall never thirst; but the water that I shall give him shall be in him a well of water springing up into everlasting life* (John 4:7,9-10,13-14).

When Jesus met the Samaritan woman at the well of Jacob, He was again moved with compassion. On this day, what He saw was a woman whose sad countenance betrayed her position as a social outcast. As a Samaritan, she was automatically set apart from the Jews she resided among. As she drew water, Jesus came near and spoke to her. In fact, He asked her for a drink of water.

She could not believe that Jesus—a Jew—would speak to a Samaritan such as she. He did not speak to her with scorn or derision. He did not attempt to intimidate her. Gently, He asked her a series of questions—questions that ultimately resulted in an answer that would satisfy her deepest thirst for all time. Jesus just kept gently pursuing this wayward sheep—this woman at the well—until it dawned on her that He himself was the Water of life.

She said, *Sir, give me this water, that I thirst not, neither come hither to draw* (John 4:15).

He said, "Go bring your husband to Me."

She answered, "I have no husband."

Jesus said, "I know."

He did not condemn her. He said, "You have been married five times, and this man you are living with now is not your husband." (See John 4:16-18.)

Then it dawned on her! This man must be the promised Messiah!

Jesus did not get hung up on preaching to a Samaritan that day, any more than this woman's gender caused Him to back away. Neither her being a woman nor a Samaritan were reasons for Jesus to back away, and we shouldn't back away today from outcasts and sinners—those modern-day "Samaritans"—that we encounter in our daily lives. We should not back off from preaching the gospel for any reason—regardless of a person's gender or political persuasion or race. Forget it! To be "politically correct" is the world's tactic, and Jesus said, "I have overcome the world."

Jesus simply sat down with this Samaritan woman at the well. He did not judge her or condemn her. He talked with her quite naturally, and she could undoubtedly sense His unconditional acceptance of her. This woman was scorned by Jews, and here was Jesus, speaking to her as if they were old acquaintances. He knew all about her sins—yet He did not call them to her attention.

There's a lesson there for those of us today who wish to win souls. The vilest sinner knows what he is doing, and he thinks about Jesus—believe me. The sinner may be actively involved in all kinds of sin, but when the Holy Ghost begins to operate and the Shepherd begins to "seek that which was lost," it's all over! The toughest sinner begins to melt, and eventually he'll come into the fold—meekly, like the mildest sheep. And from that point on, he will receive instruction from his Shepherd.

Sinners today, sheep tomorrow!
Sinners spend a lot of time thinking about God—never forget that fact. When they're in their sanest moments, they think about Him. When they're drunk, they think about Him. When they're high on drugs, they think about the Lord. And when they sleep, the sleep comes hard because their hearts are meditating on God.

God is patient. He's just waiting for these wayward sheep to come back home. He wants them in His fold. He wants to be their Shepherd. Today's sinners are tomorrow's sheep—the sheep that were scattered and are currently in want of a Shepherd. Jesus is that Shepherd. And we are the ones He has appointed to act as undershepherds to gather in that flock. We must be ready to talk to sinners about Jesus, because they can come out from under that cloud of sin at any moment and decide to live for the Lord.

The woman at the well was changed that day by a single encounter with Jesus Christ. The Word says she left her pots right there at the well—left her old lifestyle right there—and began to witness for Jesus. John 4:28-29 says, *The woman then left her waterpot, and went her way into the city, and saith to the men, Come, see a man, which told me all things that ever I did: is not this the Christ?*

But the disciples had difficulty understanding this encounter of their Master with the Samaritan woman. It's as if they had been traveling with Him for one-and-a-half years or so, and yet they still didn't get it. They saw the Samaritan woman as a sinner and not worth Jesus' time. But Jesus saw her, not as she was, but as she was destined to become.

Can you picture it? Here's Jesus with this harlot He met at a well, sitting at His feet, calling Him Lord. Next she's testifying to the crowd about His being the Messiah...and what that realization means to her. She promises to live her life for Christ, and the people who hear her testimony are giving their lives to Jesus in droves. That just didn't fit the disciples' idea of how evangelism should be conducted. So Jesus turned to the disciples and gently rebuked them, saying, *Say not ye, There are yet four months, and then cometh harvest? behold, I say unto you, Lift up your eyes, and look on the fields; for they are white already to harvest. And he that reapeth receiveth wages, and gathereth fruit unto life eternal...* (John 4:35,36).

The harvest is now!

It's the same story in this hour. The harvest is not tomorrow, or four months from now, or after you've completed a Ph.D. in evangelism. It's *now.*

Let me share the story of a young man named Paul, who came to work for me one summer. This young man was on fire for Jesus. He went on to attend Texas A & M University and is now serving the Lord in Brazil. But back then he had just received the baptism in the Holy Spirit.

During the time Paul worked for me, he began to witness to a neighbor boy who was about his age. This other boy, Lonnie, was very popular in school, and one day Paul asked me if I would mind talking to his young friend about the Lord. I said, "I'd like to, Paul, but I have an important appointment today, and I can't." About that time, the Lord arrested me and spoke to my heart, and I knew I had to skip my lunch appointment. So I said, "Yes, Paul, I'll go with you, and we'll have our talk."

The three of us sat down and just started to talk about Jesus. At the end of our talk, Lonnie prayed to give his heart to the Lord. A few days later, as Lonnie was driving to work from Hemphill to Jasper, Texas, he was involved in an accident. He was thrown from the vehicle at a speed of sixty or seventy miles per hour. His neck was broken, and he was killed instantly. I would hardly be able to live with myself today if I had resisted the Holy Ghost's leading and kept my lunch date instead of talking to Lonnie. He was ready to come into the fold—right then. As it turned out, he wouldn't have had time to get that settled later. That boy might have gone to hell if Paul and I hadn't prayed with him right then.

Be willing to see the world as sheep without a shepherd. Don't say, "Later—I'll go later." This is the day...now is the time. Go!

6
Instructed to Prosper by the Holy Ghost

> *Now we have received, not the spirit of the world, but the spirit which is of God; that we might know the things that are freely given to us of God. Which things also we speak, not in the words which man's wisdom teacheth, but which the Holy Ghost teacheth; comparing spiritual things with spiritual. But the natural man receiveth not the things of the Spirit of God: for they are foolishness unto him: neither can he know them, because they are spiritually discerned. But he that is spiritual judgeth all things, yet he himself is judged of no man.*
> —1 Corinthians 2:12-15

First Corinthians 12:14 states, *But the natural man receiveth not the things of the Spirit of God: for they are foolishness unto him: neither can he know them, because they are spiritually discerned.* The Holy Spirit is not out there trying to guide us into some kind of wild, mystical spiritual experience. No, He is our Guide. He is here for our good—to help us, to teach us, to lead us into all truth. He is here to steer us around the potholes, so to speak, and warn us of error and deception, because the things of God are spiritually discerned. The Holy Spirit is also here to instruct us in the ways of God—including how to prosper—and these ways are discerned spiritually.

Then 1 Corinthians 2:15 says, *But he that is spiritual judgeth all things, yet he himself is judged of no man.* One translation of this verse says, "He that is spiritual understands, gets insight into all things, yet he himself is not understood by anyone." That's because the carnal mind cannot comprehend spiritual things. The world just doesn't understand.

When we're born again and filled with the Holy Spirit, we become spiritual men and women. As we seek God's ways, walking in the Spirit, we begin to get spiritual insights and revelation knowledge.

However, I'm not saying that God is trying to make us into spiritual "flakes." He does not desire for us to stand out in the crowd. But when the opportunity comes to speak up for Jesus, we must be able to operate on the level of the Word and speak boldly. We must also understand that only spiritual people will be able to comprehend what the Lord is saying through us. The world can't seem to follow it, but the spiritual man or woman can understand that Word from God.

The carnal mind cannot comprehend giving

The carnal mind, for instance, just can't comprehend how giving can cause increase to come into a person's life. It does not make sense.

An accountant once told me, "Walter, it's okay for you to give away that kind of money to the church because you can get a tax write-off, and that will help a little. But there are better ways to invest it." He was speaking about Cindy's and my record of giving above our ten-percent tithe.

I said, "Thank you for the knowledge of that, because I do some of that too. But I am not going to stop giving just to feed some annuity. I'll believe God for the increase—and I will do both."

Personally, I can't think of a better investment than to give according to the Word of God. It's not a matter of how much money we have—it's what we do with what we have.

The spirit of the world vs. the Spirit of God

In 1 Corinthians 2:12, we see that there are two spirits at work on earth—the "spirit of the world" and the "Spirit of God." These two spirits operate differently in lots of ways.

The spirit of the world is based on an entirely different set of motives than the Spirit of God. The first motive of the spirit of the world asks, "What's in it for me?" It always looks out for number one because the motivation of the spirit of the world is to please the flesh.

But the motivation of the Spirit of God is to produce that which is of God. The person operating according to this Spirit will ask, "What's in it for God?" The motives of people change, but the motives of God do not change.

The Bible says that you and I have been delivered from the spirit of the world. So we should watch out for people who are operating according to the spirit of the world, and if it seems we are being conned, we should walk the other way—quickly!

Another difference between the spirit of the world and the Spirit of God has to do with goals. The goals of men and the goals of God have always been at odds. The world's goal is to accumulate a lot of material things—money, houses, cars, expensive vacations. God's goal is to get us to heaven, where we will have mansions of gold. The goal of Christians should be to do the will of God and make decisions that line up with that rather than with the world's system.

People operating by the spirit of the world make decisions based on greed, lust, fear, and feelings of inadequacy...always trying to guard their weaknesses. People who operate according to the Spirit of God do just the opposite. They make decisions from a position of strength, not weakness. They pray about their decisions and act according to the leading of the Holy Ghost. They are led by the Spirit.

In so doing, they discover that they can understand things that are impossible for the human mind to comprehend, short of the power of God. Let's take another look at verse 15: *But he that is spiritual judgeth all things, yet he himself is judged of no man.* Verse 16 adds, *For who hath known the mind of the Lord, that he may instruct him? But we have the mind of Christ.* That's powerful!

The mind of Christ, and why we need it

When I owned my own business, from time to time I would call all the sales staff in and talk to them about our products. I would make my sales people as knowledgeable as I could about what we were selling. I'd instruct them and get them excited about our product line, so they could go out there in the marketplace and sell, sell, sell. When someone asked them questions about our products, I wanted my sales force to be able to immediately respond with the right answer. In fact, I wanted them to be so knowledgeable of our product line that they would be able to speak for me out in the marketplace. I wanted them to know me and my products that well.

And the Bible says that's exactly the way we should be as Christians. We should be so full of the Word of God that we can answer immediately and account for the hope that is within us. We should know God and His Word so well that we are able to speak for Him.

But having the mind of God does not come instantly. It is not the instantaneous byproduct of salvation and the infilling of the Holy Ghost. No, the Bible says we must develop ourselves in that area. Ephesians 4:23 tells us we are to *be renewed in the spirit of* [our] *mind.* Second Corinthians 10:4,5 tells us about the weapons of our warfare: *(For the weapons of our warfare are not carnal, but mighty through God to the pulling down of strong holds;) Casting down imaginations, and every high thing that exalteth itself against the knowledge of God, and bringing into captivity every thought to the obedience of Christ. Now* we are talking about the mind of Christ! *Now* we are beginning to develop the mind of the Lord!

To have the mind of the Lord is important. If you have it, you won't be getting out there in the flesh. When you sit down and reason together with God, as we're told to do in Isaiah 1:18, you'll be talking to God on the level of the Word.

That's what Moses did!

That's what Moses did when God intended to kill all the disobedient Israelites and just start over. Moses reasoned with

God, reminding Him of His Word and His various promises. Moses said, "Don't kill them! If You do, the heathen will say that God was not able to deliver His people once He brought them out of Egypt." And God said, "All right, I won't kill them." (See Exodus 32:1-15.) Thank God, Moses sat down to reason with God, and He was so full of the Word that he knew what it said and was able to remind God of His promises to deliver His people.

Now, this does not mean that you should just go crazy and think you can tell God what to do. No, if you have the mind of Christ, you will know how to talk to God in a way that is spiritual and in keeping with His Word. You won't be caught up in carnality. You'll sit down to talk to God and He'll talk back. The Bible says, *For who hath known the mind of the Lord, that he may instruct him? But we have the mind of Christ* (1 Corinthians 2:16).

Instruction brings intimacy

The word *instruct,* as it appears in this verse, is an interesting word in that it's a Greek word that means "to unite, or to join together, or to make one." In that light, the verse may be interpreted as, "For who hath known the mind of the Lord, that he may be united with Him? But we have the mind of Christ."

That's exactly what happens when we're born again. We become united with God. We are joined together with Him. We become one with Jesus in that the same Spirit in Him—the Holy Spirit—also resides in us. We have the potential to know God intimately, if we'll take the time to get to know Him in prayer and Bible study.

But the Bible says the Lord also wants us to have the mind of Christ so that the next time the devil tries to mess with our mind, we can mess back. We have the mind of Christ—we can pray in tongues until we get wisdom. We have the mind of Christ—we can hear what God has to say. Each time the devil comes at us with a lie, we can counter with the Word of God—the truth.

You and I need to be united with God and partner with Him as co-laborers together with Christ. First Corinthians 3:9 says we are co-laborers with Christ. But you can't co-labor with Him unless you have the mind of Christ. You get the mind of Christ by studying the Word.

If we have the mind of Christ, we're going to flow in the ways of the kingdom of God. And one of those ways is to be blessed and prospered.

The revelation to prosper

When someone gets a revelation regarding prosperity, he might be poor economically at that very moment—but if God gives him something, he'll tithe it...and he'll give above the tithe. And the next time you see him, he'll have more. Then he'll give of that...and continue to be multiplied until he has achieved financial soundness.

On the other hand, there are those who say, "I'd build a church for God, but that would take a hundred thousand dollars...so I guess I can't because I don't have that much money." Forget that kind of thinking! If I had just $14.99 in my pocket and God said, "Build Me a church," I would still do my part because I know God would never tell me to do something that I could not do. He doesn't operate that way.

God's call to good stewardship

He does, however, operate according to our good stewardship. We are expected to properly steward those things God has entrusted to us. Let's look at the parable about stewardship in Luke, chapter 16:

> *There was a certain rich man, which had a steward; and the same was accused unto him that he had wasted his goods. And he called him, and said unto him, How is it that I hear this of thee? give an account of thy stewardship; for thou mayest be no longer steward. Then the steward said within himself, What shall I do? for my lord taketh away*

from me the stewardship: I cannot dig; to beg I am ashamed. I am resolved what to do, that, when I am put out of the stewardship, they may receive me into their houses.

So he called every one of his lord's debtors unto him, and said unto the first, How much owest thou unto my lord? And he said, An hundred measures of oil. And he said unto him, Take thy bill, and sit down quickly, and write fifty. Then said he to another, And how much owest thou? And he said, An hundred measures of wheat. And he said unto him, Take thy bill, and write fourscore. And the lord commended the unjust steward, because he had done wisely....

—Luke 16:1-8

Now, why is that? One day as I studied this passage, it began to dawn on me just how much stock God places in wisdom. Because he had done wisely, the steward—though unjust—was commended by his lord. The Scripture passage continues:

For the children of this world are in their generation wiser than the children of light. And I say unto you, Make to yourselves friends of the mammon of unrighteousness; that, when ye fail, they may receive you into everlasting habitations. He that is faithful in that which is least is faithful also in much: and he that is unjust in the least is unjust also in much. If therefore ye have not been faithful in the unrighteous mammon, who will commit to your trust the true riches? And if ye have not been faithful in that which is another man's, who shall give you that which is your own?

—Luke 16:8-12

What a passage of Scripture!

But I admit that for years I was stumped as far as understanding it was concerned. I tried to make some sense out of this passage, but I just didn't get it. I'd read it and begin to get into the flow of it...and then all of a sudden I'd find myself thinking, *This doesn't make sense at all! Here's this boy—out there doing what amounts to stealing—and then he is being commended for it. That doesn't sound like the God I know. I can't understand why Jesus would do that.*

Then I saw it! I began to understand that Jesus was the rich man represented in this parable. The steward represented you and me. The Church has been made the steward of the grace of God in the earth today. The steward was accused, not of stealing, but of wasting the rich man's goods. In other words, he did not use the rich man's goods properly. Since all the silver and gold on earth belong to God, it was God's goods that were being wasted by this particular steward.

If you are a person who is properly stewarding what God has given to you—if you pay your bills, pay your taxes, give your tithes and offerings and yet still increase...if you are not a person who is greedy and stores everything up, but instead are a giver—then you can expect that you will never be accused before God as an unfaithful steward. God will make you ruler over much if you have first been found faithful over little.

You may say, "How is it that God sees everything I do?" Well, if you are born again, the Spirit of God resides on the inside of you. There is virtually nothing that He does not see. He is the One who gives you the unction to do and say the things you do and say. You may say, "Well, I'm not sure I believe that." But if you are born again, you may as well believe it. It's true.

One day we will give an account

The Bible says that on judgment day, each of us will give an account for all the works we did on earth. Those works that had no worth will be burned up before the Lord as wood, hay, and stubble. Only those things with eternal value will be credited to us as gold, silver, and precious stones. One day Jesus will judge all we said, all we did, all we gave as either a work of the flesh or a work of the Spirit.

I believe the steward we read about in this parable came to the point that he realized that judgment day was near for him. He said, "What can I do? I can't dig. I can't beg. I know—I've made up my mind what I'll do!" He came to a point of decision—a turning point.

I don't know about you, but I made up my mind a long time ago what I was going to do. I decided I was going to serve God. As for me and my house, we'll serve Him.

But here's a guy who said, "I've figured out what I'm going to do." The verse reads, *I am resolved what to do, that, when I am put out of the stewardship, they may receive me into their houses* (vs.4).

Are you resolved what you will do one day...the day you die? Because, again, Jesus is not talking about earthly things, but about those things that are above. In this parable, He is talking about the steward making plans for the day he'll be received into heaven. We each need a heavenly habitation. In this parable, Jesus is teaching that what we do down here on earth will affect us eternally. We need to make plans today for entering eternity. When I saw that, I got excited.

Now, we're talking about prosperity. When God says, "Walter, it's time to give an account of your stewardship," I want to be able to respond, "Well, Lord, that first offering at Abundant Life Christian Center was for four hundred dollars. Then nine years later, we were in the middle of building a multimillion-dollar building to seat thousands. Then we acquired a million dollars' worth of television production equipment. And with it, we preached the gospel to millions of people around the globe." I want to be able to respond that way—and believe me, that's how it will be. All these things—and more—have occurred in less than ten years' time.

We can do it! It costs a penny a person to preach the gospel on television. We can do it! We *are* doing it! We're not planning on sitting here like bumps on logs, waiting for somebody else to do it. We're taking what has been given in tithes and offerings and we're investing it—in souls.

I hope to hear God say one day, "Well done, thou good and faithful *church!*"

Called to preach the gospel

God hasn't called me to straighten out the politics of America. He hasn't called me to run for office. He has called me to preach the gospel to everyone who will listen. He's called me to point the way to the door of heaven. I didn't plan on going on television. There are already enough television ministries to choose from. And they didn't get there by preaching politics. God blessed these ministries because they preached the gospel. Then some of them fell into the various traps set for them by the devil.

The devil tried to get Jesus to fall into those same traps when He was being tempted of Satan in the wilderness. But each time, Jesus countered with the Word of God, saying, "No, for it is written..." (see Matthew 4). In so doing, He avoided those traps, and God promoted Him into His public ministry. Jesus could have been a Pharisee. He was certainly well-connected by blood. He could have taken the political route. But again, He said, "No!" Politics may stroke your pride, but preaching Jesus will keep you humble.

Now, each of us needs to be wise stewards of what has been entrusted to us. We need to register and we need to vote. But the bottom line is this: *The pulpit is for the kingdom of heaven, not for politics.* Paul knew that. Once he was a chief Pharisee. Then he met Jesus, and all that changed. He was able to write, "I count it all as dung...". He gave politics up to gain *the excellency of the knowledge of Christ Jesus* (Philippians 3:8).

I make these analogies to emphasize how so many people will one day stand before Jesus to give account of their stewardship, thinking they've done all these wonderful things for Him—when in fact, those things were of little or no eternal value. Those wood, hay, and stubble things will all burn up.

If you want to play politics, I can recommend seventy-five preachers you can follow who fell into that trap. If you want to follow them, you can follow them—right into the voting booth. Preachers should lead you to an empty tomb and a living, resurrected Lord! You won't get many miracles out of a voting booth—but you'll get plenty of miracles at the feet of Jesus Christ. So why not just serve God?

The wise steward

In Luke 16:5, the steward *called every one of his lord's debtors unto him.* One translation says he "called all of his renters." In other words, he called his tenants and offered to lower their rent. Here was this steward, given charge over his lord's property, saying, "I'll cut you a deal. How much rent do you pay? I'll lower it. I'll relieve your burden, for no reason except that when I'm kicked out of my lord's house, you'll take me in. Do we have a deal?" I think that's one pretty smart guy. He's covering all the bases.

In verse 6, the debtor tells him his tab is *an hundred measures of oil. And he said unto him, Take thy bill, and sit down quickly, and write fifty.* That's like getting an immediate fifty-percent credit. *Then said he to another, And how much owest thou? And he said, An hundred measures of wheat. And he said unto him, Take thy bill, and write fourscore* [eighty] (vs.7). That's like getting a twenty-percent, on-the-spot discount just for paying cash. In essence, that's what this guy was doing—offering discounts for paying cash.

I remember when I was in business, I would offer a discount to the person who paid in cash. It was something like 1 or 1.5 percent. But I can't recall ever giving a discount as big as 20 or 50 percent. But then, I wasn't staring hell in the face, either, like this guy apparently was.

Verse 8 says, *And the lord commended the unjust steward.* He commended him because he had done wisely. He probably said something like, "If you had been that smart before and used that much wisdom, you wouldn't be in the jam you're in right now. Then Jesus made this profound statement: *For the children of this world are in their generation wiser than the children of light.*

Preparations for eternity

Now, here's what was taking place. This man was making preparations so that when his tenure as a steward ran out—for whatever reason—he would have a place to go. In other words, when he came to the end of his own abilities, at the end of his life—when he couldn't even dig his own grave—he would have someone to take him in. This is a type of what takes place at the end of each of our lives, when we must endure an inventory of all our actions.

When I read verse 8, the Holy Ghost said to me, "The world—the people of the world—are wiser with the way they use their money than Christians. They use their money better to prepare for their futures than Christians do to prepare for heaven." He said, "People who have an extremely terminal future in front of them seem to use more wisdom in preparing for their own retirements than Christians—who have eternity facing them—use their finances to prepare for heaven."

If the devil can't keep you out of heaven because you're born again, he will certainly do everything possible to keep you from getting rewards once you get there. He'll try to let you pass with the least possible rewards. He can't touch your salvation—that's not even debatable. If you believe in Jesus Christ and He is the Lord of your life, you're saved. No question about it—you'll go straight to heaven. Do not pass go, and do not collect two hundred dollars! But if the devil has anything to do with it—and he'll try—you'll get into heaven as a pauper. That's his job—to keep you from heavenly rewards.

You can get a revelation of the riches of God that are made available to you by the finished work of Calvary, and you can go to heaven as a rich man. Jesus is saying, "Make your preparations now." Just as the children of the world use their finances to prepare for their futures, so Christians must use their finances to prepare for eternity.

Look at the message of 1 Timothy 6:17-19: *Charge them that are rich in this world, that they be not highminded, nor trust in uncertain riches, but in the living God, who giveth us richly all things to enjoy; that they do good, that they be rich in good works, ready to distribute, willing to communicate; laying up in store for themselves a good foundation against the time to come, that they may lay hold on eternal life.* The Bible clearly states that the man or the woman who uses his or her finances in a godly manner will see a heavenly result.

That's because there is a spiritual counterpart to every natural reaction. That applies to everything from faith, love, and obedience to finances. As we give, the Bible says we are storing up—laying up—true riches in heaven.

Every time you give a cup of water to someone who is thirsty, the Bible says you'll receive a reward. If you bake a cake for someone, you'll be rewarded. If you take a dish of food to someone or buy groceries for a person in need, you'll be rewarded. So there are rewards for things you give and do for others, not just for the money you give. Each time you give of yourself, you are storing up a foundation against the time to come. You are laying hold of eternal life.

I get so excited when I think about that! Every act or deed that's done in faith—given out of ourselves—will one day be rewarded. We give in the natural, and we receive our rewards in the spiritual realm. Those rewards are eternal and will never be diminished. So the next time you hear a small voice saying to you, "Buy a pair of shoes for each of Bob's kids," you know you'll be rewarded if you obey. You also know that it was not the devil telling you to do that. There's no way the devil wants to see you blessed in heaven! That's the Holy Ghost telling you to minister to the needs of others—and if you do, you will be generously rewarded in heaven.

Friends of mammon?

Jesus said, in Luke 16:9, *And I say unto you, Make to yourselves friends of the mammon of unrighteousness.* What He's saying is this: "Take the mammon of unrighteousness—

money—and use it to make friends. Now, in the King James Version, that word *friend* is not the same as the way we use it, in association with buying someone's friendship. Instead, Jesus is talking about the term as "eternal habitation." He's talking about taking the money you make out there in the world's system, and using it to get somebody saved and filled with the Holy Ghost.

Remember the first thing Jesus said to Peter and Andrew when He called them as disciples? *Follow me, and I will make you fishers of men* (Matthew 4:19). He was saying, "I'll teach you how to cause people who were once at enmity with God to be friends with God and with you."

In this same sense, in Luke 16:9, Jesus was saying, "Make yourself a friend with your money, then get people saved with it." Now, the beautiful thing about using your money to get people saved is that you are not only blessing the earth with your finances and doing your part to fulfill the Great Commission, but you are laying up for yourself an incredible heavenly reward.

So verse nine could actually be interpreted like this: "Make of yourself friends of the mammon of unrighteousness—money—that when you fail—die—those you have helped to get saved will receive you into everlasting habitation—heaven." One translation of the latter part of this verse actually says, "...they will welcome you into heaven." That's powerful! It means that every time you take time to tell someone, "God loves you!" you are laying up treasure in heaven. Every time you lead someone in the sinner's prayer, or pray for their soul, you are laying up treasure in heaven. You will receive a reward. You are laying the foundation for your "everlasting habitation."

Then verse 10 states: *He that is faithful in that which is least is faithful also in much....* Giving begins today. Don't ever say, "If God would just give me a million dollars, I'd give Him a hundred thousand dollars of it!" If you don't give Him ten dollars out of every hundred that you earn right now, then you probably wouldn't give Him that hundred grand if the million dollars did come in.

You may say, "But Pastor, I don't make enough to give God anything!" And I say, "The Word says be faithful with what little you have." That's important because the verse continues: *And he that is unjust in the least is unjust also in much.*

True riches

Money is of God. It all belongs to Him. He that is faithful in the least is also faithful in much. Here God is not speaking of volume—He's talking about mammon vs. true heavenly riches. Money is the "little"—eternal riches are the "much." So if you have been faithful with money—the least of God's riches—you will be entrusted later, in heaven, with the true riches.

Let's talk for a moment about those true riches. What are they? The Bible says the true riches include revelation knowledge of the Word of God and things like peace, joy, and the gifts of the Spirit—things that are of great value but things which money cannot buy. Money, after all, is simply that which tests the will of men toward God. And if a man is faithful with his money, then he will be faithful with spiritual things.

Verse 12 continues: *And if ye have not been faithful in that which is another man's, who shall give you that which is your own?* I often hear people say things like, "I want to be in full-time ministry..." and "I've got this vision..." and "I want to be a preacher...." But I watch and see that these individuals are not being faithful where God has planted them. They can't attend church two times a week, much less three times. They don't pay their tithes. They won't work in the nursery, either...or do any other volunteer work. They are not being faithful with another man's vision. How can they ever hope to see their own vision come to pass? So they stay frustrated, waiting for their ship to come in spiritually. And God is saying, "It's at the door, but you've got to do your part first with another man's ministry. If you'll be faithful with that, then I'll commit to you your own."

God said to Abraham, "I will bless you, and you will be a blessing." He's saying that to you and me. How we do our part will either bring those blessings forth or keep them "at the door"—just out of reach.

7
Give Bountifully, Not Sparingly

There's a major difference between the word *sparingly* and the beautiful word, *bountifully*. *Sparingly* is what you'll reap if you give sparingly. But *bountifully* is what you'll reap if you give bountifully. When you give sparingly, you'll reap a lifestyle of just getting by. But if you give bountifully, you'll reap a lifestyle of having more than enough.

The Greek word for *sparingly* means "grudgingly." Those who sow stingily, or grudgingly, will barely have enough to get by. But that word *bountiful* is truly a beautiful word. Literally, it means "repetitious, continual abundance of giving." It means that the person who gives to God bountifully—openly, willingly, freely—will reap from Him more than enough.

The alabaster box

Two nights before Jesus was crucified, He sat in the home of Simon the leper—or should I say, Simon the ex-leper—and was ministered to by a woman who poured upon His head the expensive ointment kept in an alabaster box. This woman gave bountifully to the Lord. As we study the account in the Gospels of Matthew, Mark, and Luke, we see just how bountiful a gift she gave:

> *Now when Jesus was in Bethany, in the house of Simon the leper, there came unto him a woman having an alabaster box of very precious ointment, and poured it on his head, as he sat at meat. But when his disciples saw it, they had indignation, saying, To what purpose is this waste? For this ointment might have been sold for much, and given to the poor. When Jesus understood it, he said unto*

> them, Why trouble ye the woman? for she hath wrought a good work upon me. For ye have the poor always with you; but me ye have not always. For in that she hath poured this ointment on my body, she did it for my burial. Verily I say unto you, Wheresoever this gospel shall be preached in the whole world, there shall also this, that this woman hath done, be told for a memorial of her.
> —Matthew 26:6-13

What a beautiful story! Here was a woman, so moved by the ministry of the Messiah, that she spent an exorbitant amount of money to buy an alabaster box filled with expensive ointment. As the precious spikenard (fragrant ointment) ran from Jesus' head down to His feet, the woman wept and began to wash His feet with her tears. Then she dried His feet with her beautiful long hair. (See the account of this event in Luke 7:36-50.)

The Word says that ointment was *very precious*. This Greek terminology means "expensive, or costly." Just two days before His death on the cross, the Lord was sitting in the home of a man He had healed of leprosy, having costly ointment poured onto His head. While the scribes and Pharisees were plotting His demise, here was Jesus being entertained lavishly.

While this was going on, the scribes and Pharisees stood nearby, murmuring against the display of extravagance being directed at Jesus. Jesus was ridiculed for receiving such an expensive gift, and the woman was criticized for giving it. She had no motive in giving such an expensive gift, other than that she had the revelation to do it.

Religion today is still trying to do all it can to snuff out the revelation of Jesus Christ on earth today. But Jesus Christ is still in the business of taking people's lives and changing them.

When Jesus met Simon, he was an outcast and a leper. Two nights before the crucifixion of Jesus, Simon was an ex-leper...lavishly entertaining his Lord.

That's how it is today. Jesus changes the drug addict into an ex-drug addict...the alcoholic into an ex-alcoholic...the poor man into an ex-poor man who becomes rich in Christ. And then He fellowships with them.

But even in biblical times, it was unusual to have an entire box of spikenard used to anoint one person. Think about how much an alabaster box filled with spikenard may have cost in those days. It may have cost this woman everything she had, but she broke the box open and poured its contents onto Jesus' head. For this woman, that was the same as breaking the bank.

She broke the bank and poured the precious ointment onto His head! I said, "Glory to God!" when I realized that. I realized too that the Holy Ghost is still taking our gifts and multiplying them and pouring them back into our lives as blessings.

Crowned and anointed

I think this woman was actually crowning Jesus as Lord. The Word says she was chastised for her ministrations to Him that night because her gift was so elaborate and expensive. The Bible says its worth was *three hundred pence* (Mark 14:5).

This woman began to weep as she ministered to the Lord. She cried, "I'm a sinner." But the Lord responded mercifully, "Woman, thy sins are many but they are forgiven this day." She was crowning Him as Lord, but she was also anointing Him for a mighty work—the crucifixion that was soon to take place.

Now, this was no penny-ante offering. This woman was poor, and three hundred pence was the equivalent in biblical times of one to two years' wages. In those days, that amount would have been equal to several hundred thousand dollars. According to today's currency, it would be worth about fifty thousand dollars.

This tender-hearted woman broke the bank, so to speak, to buy that expensive ointment that signified Jesus' preparation for burial—and then she brought it to Him. We don't even know her name, but her offering was more precious than any other offering to Jesus ever recorded in the Bible.

Outrageous generosity

This woman's gift was extraordinarily generous, since just a little spikenard would have been enough to anoint Jesus and release a sweet-smelling perfume into His clothes and skin that would last for days. Spikenard is a very powerful, fragrant ointment. Just a little bit of spikenard would have been considered to be a luxurious gift.

But the woman brought an entire box of costly spikenard, and used all of it to anoint the Lord two nights before His crucifixion. No wonder the scribes and Pharisees—and even some of the disciples—thought the gift was simply too extravagant. Here was an example of outrageous generosity if there ever was one.

I can just picture the stern-faced Pharisees murmuring among themselves, shaking their heads with their displeasure, and asking, "Woman, what are you doing?" And I can imagine her reply: "I don't know—all I know is God told me to do this!"

Yet many of those present thought such extravagance was wasteful, and they spoke against the woman, saying the ointment shouldn't be wasted but should be sold and the money given to the poor.

But Jesus said, "Let her alone. Why trouble you her? She has wrought a good work on Me. You will have the poor with you always, and whenever you will you may do them good. But Me you will not have always...." One translation of this passage says, "But you don't always have an opportunity to do something for God." *She hath done what she could...* (Mark 14:7).

Do what you can!

I was reading this passage of Scripture one day, when the Lord began to speak to me about how some people live all their lives, talking about what they can and cannot do. Jesus said this woman did what she could. She stopped living on the level of "can't," and took what action she could to bless the Lord before His crucifixion ended His earthly ministry.

If you believe you can't, you *can't*. You're living on the level of can't. But if you believe you can, you'll find there are all sorts of things you can do—and most of those things begin with a decision to do what you can for Jesus.

Why did this woman do what she did? Because God told her to do it—and because she believed she could do it! In other words, she got a revelation to do it!

The anointing that breaks the yoke

According to the Word, this woman came to the home of Simon the leper with a very specific assignment. She came with an alabaster box full of expensive ointment to anoint Jesus for burial.

Now, the Bible says the anointing breaks the yoke! *The yoke shall be destroyed because of the anointing* (Isaiah 10:27). She doused the Lord with anointing oil that was worth three hundred pence. Two days later, Judas sold Him into captivity for a handful of silver—also worth three hundred pence, to be exact. (See Matthew 26:14,15.)

While Jesus was all alone in the Garden of Gethsemane, sweating blood and praying fervently about the torment He would go through in a matter of hours, it was the anointing that carried Him through. As He agonized on His knees, praying that the cup of death be passed from Him "if it was God's will," I can just imagine a breeze blowing through the cedar and olive trees, capturing some of that sweet-smelling perfume that lingered on His clothes and causing its fragrance to waft into Jesus' nostrils as an encouragement that the anointing was there for what He was about to do.

A few moments later, Roman soldiers arrived with members of the Sanhedrin and Judas—who betrayed Him with a kiss (see Matthew 26:36-50). But the anointing was already on Him. The soldiers could smell it as they reached out to arrest Him. Judas could smell it as he leaned forward to kiss His cheek.

The anointing was already on Him! And the anointing was greater than the betrayal. It was greater than Jesus' captivity. It was greater than His crucifixion. When they took Him down from the cross and wrapped His body in linen, that fragrance of spikenard was still on Him—it had to be. That's strong stuff, and He had just had a whole box of it poured out on Him. The embalming process only heaped on more oil and spices. Then they laid Him in the grave and rolled the stone across its opening. But the anointing was even greater than that!

A sweet savor

The fragrance of the spikenard is a type of the Holy Ghost. Any time you encounter the word *fragrance* in the Bible, it's a metaphor for the Holy Spirit. Jesus took that sweet-smelling fragrance with Him as He descended into hell. Nothing smells good there—not hatred, not murder, not adultery, not extortion, not lying.

In hell, there was just the stench of sin mixed with burning flesh and putridness. But Jesus took the anointing with Him to hell—conquering sin and death! He went to where the demons ruled—demons of AIDS, demons of cancer, demons of fear, demons of poverty, demons of all types of mystical cults and false religions—and He conquered them!

All those fallen angels—now demons—cast out of heaven along with Lucifer, were trying to reach out and grab Jesus and keep Him there. But the anointing breaks the yoke, and hell and all its demons—not even Satan himself—could hold Him there.

The anointing began to flow and the demons had to flee. Jesus then took the keys to hell and death, and on the third day rose from the grave to the astonishment of everyone—even His mother and Mary Magdalene and His closest disciples. (See Matthew 28:1-10.)

A memorial of the woman

All of this occurred after one poor women took all she had and invested it in an expensive box of spikenard to anoint Jesus for burial. She was so insignificant a figure in her city that her name is not even listed. We don't know who she was—but God does. The Word says, "Wherever the gospel is preached in all the world, what this woman has done shall be told as a memorial of her" (see Matthew 26:13).

The word *memorial* as used in this verse literally means "this is a sign...this is what took place...this is how it happened." So Jesus was saying, "The gospel shall be preached in all the earth, and this is how it will happen. If no one else will answer the call, God will move upon little, no-name poor women, and they will come and give what they have so the gospel can be preached on the earth, and then the anointing will be released."

God wants us to prosper so we can do our part in our generation to take the gospel and to release the anointing around the world. He doesn't want us to spend everything we have to buy a box of spikenard, but He does want us to do what we can for Jesus' sake because the time is short before His glorious return.

And the price is not cheap—it costs something. But how much is a soul worth these days? The money to take the gospel around the globe is going to have to come from somewhere, and it's going to have to come from you and me.

Blessed...to be a blessing

The Lord doesn't want us to just live from paycheck to paycheck. He wants us to have more than enough to meet our needs. That's how it was with Abraham. God blessed him, multiplied him, and raised him up to father a mighty nation. Abraham didn't have that old-time confession—"I'm poor, but I'm proud!" No, he was not poor because God blessed him. He then *became* a blessing.

In Genesis 12:2, God said, *...I will bless thee, and make thy name great; and thou shalt be a blessing.* "I will bless you, and you will be a blessing"—that's still God's promise to us, as children of Abraham. He wants to bless you and me today because we can't *be* a blessing until we're *blessed.*

Abraham was blessed...and his son Isaac was blessed. The Bible says that when Isaac was blessed, there was a famine in the land. Even though he sowed in times of famine, he received a hundred-fold return on his seed. He reaped a hundred fold. Isaac reaped what he did because Abraham had been wise enough to teach his son how to tithe and make offerings before the Lord. Even in times of drought, God can make things favor those who favor Him.

Abraham's descendants were taught to tithe, but eventually each one of them received a personal revelation regarding tithing. As they began to operate in that personal revelation, Abraham's son Isaac and Isaac's son Jacob were blessed. In fact, they grew very rich.

If you give one dime to God out of every dollar you have and keep the other nine dimes, He will give you back sometimes thirty, sometimes sixty, and sometimes a hundred times more than you gave. That's what I call prosperity!

Be careful not to bind prosperity

The sad part is, some people bind up prosperity by the words of their mouths, by not tithing, or by refusing to obey God. They are full of greed and don't use their money to serve God as well as to supply their own need. They use their money strictly selfishly. They're stingy. Every now and then, they toss God a few bucks, but they keep most of what they earn for themselves. When that happens, these people are binding on earth what God has actually loosed for them in heaven—prosperity. They're binding it away.

Isaiah 1:19 states, *If ye be willing and obedient, ye shall eat the good of the land.* There are Christians today who give their tithes, yet they still don't eat the good of the land. Why is that? Because they're not obedient. They tithe, but they still worry and live in turmoil and torment regarding their personal finances. They have a heart for God, yet they don't seem to understand that obedience for its own sake is legalism. Anyone can keep a bunch of laws, but the Bible says the law "frustrates grace" (see Galatians 2:21). The law makes grace to no avail. So we must be both willing *and* obedient—then we will eat the good of the land. Isaiah 1:19 indicates that a willing heart goes right along with an obedient heart. When we're both willing and obedient, we will be giving out of a correct spirit—then God will cause us to eat the good of the land.

All financial blessings stem from God

One thing we must always remember is that at all times, our finances come from God. The Word specifically states that God "owns all the cattle on a thousand hills" (see Psalm 50:10), that *the silver is mine, and the gold is mine, saith the Lord of hosts* (Haggai 2:8), and that *the earth is the Lord's, and the fulness thereof* (1 Corinthians 10:26). These and other similar scriptures all mean just one thing: All financial blessings stem from God. That's why it's so important that we give Him the glory and thank Him each time He blesses us financially.

Every paycheck is a blessing from God. We must rejoice in that by saying, "Thank You, God, for blessing me with this paycheck" and by giving Him back the tithe. Those who are in business should thank God for every business deal that comes along, with the understanding that every penny of profit from the business that comes in the door comes from God.

We must learn to tithe obediently and also to give bountifully, not sparingly, to the work of God. For then we will reap a reward from God that is more than enough to meet our needs.

8
God Commands the Blessings Upon His People

God can cause blessings to come into your life miraculously. Did you know He can command the blessing to come upon your life? You may think you need a couple of college degrees to prosper in life, but I've got news for you: What you need is for God to command the blessing! You don't have to have a college degree to be blessed by God or even to be promoted by Him.

Part of what God is doing in this new move of the Holy Spirit on earth today is commanding the blessing upon His people. He is causing blessings to come upon His people from all directions—even unexpectedly. The blessings are coming because He is commanding them to come forth.

Just as He commanded quail to be sent to His people during their forty-year wanderings in the wilderness (see Exodus 16:13), and just as He commanded the ravens to feed the prophet Elijah by the brook, Cherith (see 1 Kings 17:4), so He is commanding blessings upon His people today. He is doing it so the move of God on earth can be sustained. Someone has to finance the work of God on earth—and that "someone" must be you and me. When a move of God takes place, the blessings begin to flow. Why? So God can sustain it.

God has always had a means of sustaining His plan, and it has usually come through people. However, if necessary, He will send manna from heaven...ravens to feed a worn-out servant...water from a rock. God is not limited to using people to sustain His plan, but often it has been humans that He used.

There is an example of this to be found in the story of the widow woman who took what she had from her meager food supply in times of famine and fed the prophet Elijah. She was down to the last of the meal and oil. In fact, she had just enough to bake a small cake for herself and her son. And then—certain starvation. But God told the prophet:

> *Arise, get to Zarephath, which belongeth to Zidon, and dwell there: behold, I have commanded a widow woman there to sustain thee.*
>
> *So he arose and went to Zarephath. And when he came to the gate of the city, behold, the widow woman was there gathering of sticks: and he called to her, and said, Fetch me, I pray thee, a little water in a vessel, that I may drink. And as she was going to fetch it, he called to her, and said, Bring me, I pray thee, a morsel of bread in thine hand.*
>
> *And she said, As the Lord thy God liveth, I have not a cake, but an handful of meal in a barrel, and a little oil in a cruse: and, behold, I am gathering two sticks, that I may go in and dress it for me and my son, that we may eat it, and die.*
>
> *And Elijah said unto her, Fear not; go and do as thou hast said: but make me thereof a little cake first, and bring it unto me, and after make for thee and for thy son. For thus saith the Lord God of Israel, The barrel of meal shall not waste, neither shall the cruse of oil fail, until the day that the Lord sendeth rain upon the earth.*
>
> *And she went and did according to the saying of Elijah: and she, and he, and her house, did eat many days.*
>
> —1 Kings 17:9-15

But even before the prophet met the widow woman at Zarephath, God said to Elijah, *I have commanded a widow woman there to sustain thee* (vs.9).

God prepares the way

What amazes me is that God had already spoken to this woman and prepared her to give what she had to Elijah. She could have said, "No—that's all I have! You can't have my last piece of bread!" But she was both willing and obedient and gave what she had to the prophet. And as a result, God caused her barrel of meal and cruse of oil to be continually full—a miracle that fed her and the members of her household for three years!

I can just picture the expressions on her friends' faces as she told them of how her meal barrel just kept filling up day after day...and how no matter how much oil she used, the cruse remained full! Her life, no doubt, became a living testimony in this season of drought and starvation. She and her son were eating cakes every day, when those around them were wondering where the next morsel of food would come from. This poor widow woman actually had enough meal and oil left over at the end of the day that sometimes her son would take the excess into town and sell it. That's prosperity!

Why did this miracle of more than enough take place? Because this widow woman was willing and obedient, and because God commanded the blessing.

Willing and obedient

If you trust God and obey Him with a willing heart, you'll prosper also. If you are a good steward with what you have and move out from under that fear, God will command a blessing to come to you. God wants your life to be a testimony of His ability to prosper you. He wants your life to reflect the truth of Philippians 4:19: *My God shall supply all your need according to his riches in glory by Christ Jesus.*

God can command the blessing upon you in all sorts of ways. Perhaps you'll receive a promotion. Perhaps you'll get a lot of overtime. Maybe you'll change jobs and get a better one...with better pay and benefits. Or He may create a job—just for you, out of nothing—and continue to speak your name to the boss until he obeys and hires you to fill it.

When God commands the blessing, He causes your life to be a witness to others. He wants you to be blessed, but He also wants your motivations to be right ones so that you will properly steward those blessings. He wants you to make more money, but not just so you can spend more money. Money is a great deceiver. It does not satisfy. And in some instances, it can actually pull you away from the plan of God for your life. And if you're gullible enough and carnal enough, the devil will actually make you an offer you can't refuse. He'll pull you right away from your destiny, and he'll use money to do it.

The goose that may have laid the golden egg
I'll give you an example from my own life. When Cindy and I were first married, I was offered a manager's position at the mill where I worked. Since I was just twenty-four and Cindy and I had only been married for two years, the bigger job and extra money sounded pretty tempting. But I said, "Sounds great to me, but I think I'll just pray about it." So I went home and prayed about the job and couldn't get any peace in my spirit. Finally I heard the Lord speak: "Walter, if you take that job, you're going to miss the plan of God for your life." So I turned it down.

It sure looked like I'd missed the goose that was laying the golden egg. But a few days later, the Holy Ghost spoke to me again and said, "You're going to get another job offer."

Soon after that, a man walked up to me while I was in a store and offered me a fantastic job. This man was a millionaire, and I was intimidated by him. I had no more considered going to work for him than the man in the moon. In fact, I said, "Thank you—I'm flattered, but...." I couldn't wait to get out of there! The man scared me to death, just being around him. A few days later, the Holy Ghost said, "Go take that job!"

This job proved to be a better opportunity than the manager's job at the mill, and God bountifully supplied our need—even though at times I wasn't sure where I was going. I didn't follow money, I followed the leading of the Holy Ghost. From the minute that new door opened, God began to bless our lives financially. God commanded the blessing, and Cindy and I were promoted into a new financial realm. We were led by the Spirit. We obeyed God, and he commanded the blessing upon our lives.

What "rich" is...
Now, I'm not saying that God will make everybody millionaires. The Scripture doesn't say that. But God wants to make you rich. Let me tell you what "rich" is: *Rich is having more money than you have bills. Rich means every time you have a need, you also have a supply.* Well, if that's rich, I'll take it!

But God will make some people millionaires—even multimillionaires—in these end times, and He can do it in an instant. You can take a gun along on an outdoor stroll, shoot it into the ground, and bubbling up will come crude—"Texas tea." Now, it may not happen just like that—but this is an example of the "suddenness" in which God can change things during this move of God on earth today.

He wants to promote the gospel throughout the earth, and those who are willing and obedient to take it there, God will bless. He will raise them up. He will even make some of them multimillionaires. After all, how much is just one soul worth? The answer is simple: Just one soul is worth the blood of Jesus. Jesus died for every sinner who ever lived, and if that had been reduced to just one person, still He would have made the sacrifice on the cross of Calvary.

That's how serious God is about souls.

He's so serious that He gave His most precious gift—His Son (see John 3:16).

The parable of the talents
In Matthew 25, we learn the parable of the man who traveled to a far country. In this lesson about the kingdom of heaven, relating the principle of the talents, we read:

For the kingdom of heaven is as a man travelling into a far country, who called his own servants, and delivered unto them his goods, and unto one he gave five talents, to another two, and to another one; to every man according to his several ability; and straightway took his journey. Then he that had received the five talents went and traded with the same, and made them other five talents. And likewise he that had received two, he also gained other two. But he that had received one went and digged in the earth, and hid his lord's money.

After a long time the lord of those servants cometh, and reckoneth with them. And so he that had received five talents came and brought other five talents, saying, Lord, thou deliveredst unto me five talents: behold, I have gained beside them five talents more. His lord said unto him, Well done, thou good and faithful servant: thou hast been faithful over a few things, I will make thee ruler over many things: enter thou into the joy of thy lord.

He also that had received two talents came and said, Lord, thou deliveredst unto me two talents: behold, I have gained two other talents beside them. His lord said unto him, Well done, good and faithful servant; thou hast been faithful over a few things, I will make thee ruler over many things: enter thou into the joy of thy lord.

Then he which had received the one talent came and said, Lord, I knew thee that thou art an hard man, reaping where thou hast not sown, and gathering where thou hast not strowed; and I was afraid, and went and hid thy talent in the earth: lo, there thou hast that is thine. His lord answered and said unto him, Thou wicked and slothful servant, thou knewest that I reap where I sowed not, and gather where I have not strowed: Thou oughtest therefore to have put my money to the exchangers,

and then at my coming I should have received mine own with usury. Take therefore the talent from him, and give it unto him which hath ten talents. For unto every one that hath shall be given, and he shall have abundance: but from him that hath not shall be taken away even that which he hath. And cast ye the unprofitable servant into outer darkness: there shall be weeping and gnashing of teeth.
—Matthew 25:14-30

This fascinating parable contains many truths. In it, God begins to contrast the kingdom of God with the world's system. In the parable, God gives His servants different talents—gifts, abilities—in different measures. Then it is their responsibility to properly steward those talents, gifts, and abilities. That's how it was in biblical times, and that's how it is yet today.

One day as I was studying this parable, the Lord began to show me that there are many people in the church who have been blessed with more than others, yet they have engineered their lives according to the world's system and not God's kingdom. And the Lord said, "God's system is contrary to the world's system—so don't hook up with it."

To stay on God's system, He wants us to take one-tenth of everything we have and give it to Him. Then we're to keep the remaining nine-tenths. Anything we give beyond that is up to us—an offering. But the tithe is the first ten percent of what we have.

God wants to see us multiply

However, God desires more than just our tithes and offerings. He wants us to take the money we have left and watch it multiply, because how we use what's left becomes a test of our faithfulness to Him.

Now, I am not a millionaire, but neither am I a poor man. Cindy and I live well. And that's what God intends. If we live well, we will be examples to those who have never had such an image in front of them that serving God can cause them to live well and prosper. Then we'll see their standard of living come right on up as they get into the flow of what God has for them. And that happens by the principles regarding money and its use that are contained in this parable in Matthew 25.

Part of investing those talents is winning souls. If the Holy Ghost is in you, and if you've been faithful with those talents, you'll win souls and enter into the joy of the Lord. Then one day you'll be able to hear the Lord say, "Well done...."

Don't get me wrong—there are trials and tribulations involved in this life, and there is a price to be paid. I don't want to minimize this in any way, because there are those around the world who have died in prisons and been tortured and martyred for their faith. They pay an extreme price to take the gospel to their neighbors and loved ones.

But I want to talk about the "joy" side of it. I don't want to stand up and talk about what the devil did to me—I just want to talk about the joy that comes from being found faithful over little, and the promotion that comes when God pronounces that we're ready to be made "faithful over much." Our mandate, then, is to increase the portion God has allotted to us so we will be able to increase our ability to use wisely what has been entrusted to us here on earth.

In Proverbs 3:16, God states that if we use wisdom in our finances, we will reap two things: Length of days in our right hand, and riches and honor in the other. This is very interesting, in this day when people everywhere seek methods of prolonging the aging process and staying young. The Word is specific: Honor the Lord, honor your parents, walk upright before Him, keep the commandments. In other words, live on the level of the Word and you will prosper and lengthen your life span.

We are the free-thinking crowd of the sixties, a generation in which everyone has been affected by one of the primary philosophies of the day—humanism. We're the ones who are so smart, and so full of greed that we are too smart for God. And for a while, it looked like an entire generation—the flower people—would be lost.

But the Holy Ghost broke through, and waves of evangelism began to sweep through this age group—the boomers. Now we're the generation with the potential and the capacity to preach the gospel to every living creature on the planet. The technology is now in place to reach everyone, and people are getting saved by the millions right now on planet earth. And of those millions, thousands are being raised up who will preach in pulpits that haven't even been built yet. And they won't just be coming to the United States to do it—they're going to preach to the four corners of the earth.

Not everyone is called in this hour to stand in a pulpit in Papua, New Guinea to preach. But everyone is called in this hour to be a faithful steward and do their part to finance the work done around the globe for Jesus.

Whether it's with one, two, five, or ten talents, everyone is called to do his or her part. Then look what God says, after a person is found faithful over a little: "I will make you ruler over many things." What are some of those things? How about fear, poverty, doubt and unbelief, racial prejudice, all kinds of division and strife, ignorance of the Word of God, sickness, lack—all those things that have been holding you down all your life. Those are the things God will make you ruler over.

It reminds me of those who say, "I'd like to serve God, but I would have to give up too many things."

Well, that's true: You're going to have to give up sinning. You're going to have to give up fear, sickness, doubt, poverty, and all those things you've been shackled to for your entire life. Isn't that a shame?

God says, "I will make you ruler over many things."

But the servant who received one talent could not get the vision for putting his talent to work. He couldn't get past fear, doubt, and unbelief. So he chose to believe a lie instead of the truth, and he buried his talent and became known as a man who robbed God. Here was a man who jumped to all the wrong conclusions about the Lord, stating, "I know You're a hard man, and that You've reaped where You've not sown." He had started to form his own religious ideas about God, and moved on to falsely accuse Him.

Sowing and reaping is found throughout the Word

The Bible is all about sowing and reaping, so where did this man get the idea that God did not conform to those same principles? After all, He's the one who set the plan in motion!

God sowed the ultimate seed—His Son. He sowed His Word, and when that seed falls on the earth, it causes a crop to come up. The Word produces fruit. Yet here was this unjust servant, claiming that God did not sow! That's exactly what people do when they are not faithful in their finances. They alter their doctrines a little bit to justify themselves for not using their talents the way God said they should be used. But when it comes right down to it, they have just one excuse— the same one as the unfaithful servant in this parable of the talents: "I was afraid...."

Even in the face of fear, there's an answer in the Word. Serve God first with your finances, and fear will leave. It will go right out the window. Here's how to break fear: The next time you start to give something in the offering, open your wallet or purse and look inside. If there's a five-dollar bill, a ten-dollar bill, and a one-dollar bill, reach for the ten. Then put it in the offering plate while the devil is chattering, "You may not have enough money to buy food!" Just put that ten in the offering plate and say to the devil, "You're a liar!"

Think about this: The one who had received the smallest amount was the one who failed with money—not the one who received ten talents. A lot of times we think, "That's how it is with rich people—they're so stingy!" In reality, it's the rich man who is often the most generous giver and the one with little resources who retains what he should have given to God.

In the example of the parable of the talents, the Lord did not look at the unfaithful servant with sympathy. He called him, "wicked and slothful." Then He took what the man had and gave it to a more faithful steward.

God does not judge the amount of our giving—the amount has nothing to do with it. He judges our faithfulness with what we have been given, because all things belong to Him to begin with.

Neither should those who have been entrusted with more riches get over into pride and begin to look down on those who don't have as much. That's another way to lose ground financially. God says that everyone who has will be given more. Those who have been faithful—those who have walked uprightly before God, who have served God with their talents—will be given more, and they shall have abundance.

9
The House of God: The Storehouse

Another reason God wants us to prosper is so we can build households of faith, houses of God—churches. I saw that one day as I was studying the Book of Ezra. In it, God said He "moved upon the spirit of the people" to build His house. That's when the Spirit of God spoke to my spirit: "I have put the spirit of a builder upon you, and you will build for Me all the days of your life!" I got so excited when I heard the Lord say that, I didn't know what to do. The spirit of a builder: That's powerful, considering Jesus was a carpenter.

In Hebrews 11:10, Abraham looked for a city whose builder and maker was God. He looked for a city that was built without hands. The Greek word for *builder* comes from *archetecton,* and from it, we get the meanings "chief architect" and "chief builder." I believe Jesus came as a carpenter to signify His position as chief architect—builder and creator of everything. In John, chapter 1, it says there was nothing made that was not made by Him. So by that, we can trace Jesus all the way back to the Garden of Eden.

God wants us to prosper so we can build churches—houses of His righteousness...storehouses—in the name of Jesus, the chief architect and builder.

Jacob builds a house of God

In a dramatic desert encounter with God that took place during a dream, Jacob got the revelation to both build a house of God and perpetuate it with his tithes and offerings. Genesis 28:10-17 says:

> *And Jacob went out from Beersheba, and went toward Haran. And he lighted upon a certain place, and tarried there all night, because the sun was set; and he took of the stones of that place, and put them for his pillows, and lay down in that place to sleep. And he dreamed, and behold a ladder set up on the earth, and the top of it reached to heaven: and behold the angels of God ascending and descending on it. And, behold, the Lord stood above it, and said, I am the Lord God of Abraham thy father, and the God of Isaac: the land whereon thou liest, to thee will I give it, and to thy seed; And thy seed shall be as the dust of the earth, and thou shalt spread abroad to the west, and to the east, and to the north, and to the south: and in thee and in thy seed shall all the families of the earth be blessed.*
>
> *And, behold, I am with thee, and will keep thee in all places whither thou goest, and will bring thee again into this land; for I will not leave thee, until I have done that which I have spoken to thee of. And Jacob awaked out of his sleep, and he said, Surely the Lord is in this place; and I knew it not. And he was afraid, and said, How dreadful is this place! this is none other but the house of God, and this is the gate of heaven.*

This event represented a turning point in the life of a man known as a schemer and a manipulator. Although he loved God thoroughly, Jacob was often ruled by his own iniquities. Consequently, he was always taking one step forward and two steps back. That is, until he had this powerful experience with God in the middle of the desert.

He could not get onto the right track until he had that dream and saw the ladder descending from heaven, with the angels of God moving up and down it. Jacob was so moved by the dream that early the next morning, he *took the stone that he had put for his pillows, and set it up for a pillar* (a cornerstone), *and poured oil upon the top of it* (vs.18) in what he proclaimed to be the house of God. This is the first time in the Bible that we see the anointing poured out like that, as oil. Jacob poured the oil—a type of the anointing—onto the rock—a type of Jesus. And, thank God, that's still how we're getting it! The anointing comes in the Person of Jesus, and then He just pours it on!

The place of seed

In Genesis 28:19, Jacob *called the name of that place Bethel: but the name of that city was called Luz at the first.* Now, there's an interesting word—*luz*. In Hebrew, it literally means "a tree that produces nuts." Perhaps it is referring to an almond tree or some other type of nut-bearing tree. But as I studied this passage of Scripture one day, the Holy Ghost reminded me, "Nuts are seeds!" So Jacob went to that place named "seed," and renamed it "Bethel," which means "the house of God." And the house of God is still the place of seed in the life of the believer.

In Malachi 3:10, when God says, *Bring ye all the tithes into the storehouse, that there may be meat in mine house...,* the Hebrew word for "meat" also means "seed." So the house of God is not only the place of seed, but it's the place of perpetual seed where the anointing is poured out. The God we serve—who is the same yesterday, today, and tomorrow—is still calling His house a place of seed—and out of it springs fruit for our lives. God wants our lives to be fruit-bearing.

It was there at Bethel that Jacob got the vision for giving to God. *And Jacob vowed a vow, saying, If God will be with me, and will keep me in this way that I go, and will give me bread to eat, and raiment to put on, so that I come again to my father's house in peace; then shall the Lord be my God: and this stone, which I have set for a pillar, shall be God's house: and of all that thou shalt give me I will surely give the tenth unto thee* (Genesis 28:20-22).

It's going to take money!

What we're building—the church of God on earth—is going to take money, and God can provide it. God will build us a house, and He will cause it to prosper so that we can build *Him* a house. He wants us to have nice houses and to pay all our bills. But beyond that, He wants us to build His house because the local New Testament church is God's plan for the restoration of humanity. The New Testament church is the place of protection against deception in the earth today. There are many deceiving spirits, all with voices, religions, and doctrines designed to confuse and lead God's flock away from the truth of the gospel. The New Testament church is the place of protection against these dangerous end-time influences because that is where the Word of God is constantly taught.

The Word is the only constant in this era we're living in. It's the only thing that will last. The earth will eventually pass away, but God's Word will not pass away (see Mark 13:31).

If we want the same manifestations of God's glory that were present in the early church on the day of Pentecost—if we want that same anointing—we're going to have to stay on the level of the same Word that was preached then. The Word has been constant since creation, and it will always remain the same. We need the Word of God—all of it, Old and New Testaments. Did you know there are churches today that don't believe in teaching from the Old Testament. I can't find that anywhere in the Bible. The Old Testament teaches us about the nature of God and His concern for mankind. And while we don't find New Testament-type demonstrations of the operation of the Holy Spirit, there are many accounts of miracles and signs and wonders. The Word says we must stir up our minds toward both the old and the new. Neither should we rely on teachings from the Old Testament only, but examine the whole Word of God for its truth.

Perhaps this is what Peter was addressing when he wrote, *...there shall come in the last days scoffers, walking after their own lusts, and saying, Where is the promise of his coming? for* *since the fathers fell asleep, all things continue as they were from the beginning of the creation* (2 Peter 3:3-4).

Verse 5 continues, *For this they willingly are ignorant of, that by the word of God the heavens were of old, and the earth standing out of the water and in the water.* From this, we see there must have been conflicting philosophies in that day about creation, as there are today. Men have always had their own ideas and opinions regarding the things of God, and what was called Gnosticism in biblical times is known as humanism today.

Seminaries in the United States and throughout the world are certainly not immune from gnostic-like deception. In fact, from some seminaries are emerging doctrines that are not even biblical. These teachings have caused many to stumble by watering down the Word and compromising its true intent. The Word of God will set us free—unless it's been tampered with by man's doctrines and the deception of the age.

Why is the Word so important to the believer? Because it takes the Word to get faith—and without faith, it is impossible to please God (see Hebrews 11:6). So all the devil has to do to get you out of faith is keep you away from the place where the Word is taught. If he can do that, then he has accomplished his objective. If you don't hear the Word preached often, your sword will become disarmed, and perhaps eventually be stolen.

The Church: A place of study

The church is not the only place where you'll get the Word. You must also read it for yourself. Read the Bible, study its contents, and, as Paul told Timothy, *Study to show thyself approved unto God, a workman that needeth not to be ashamed, rightly dividing the word of truth* (2 Timothy 2:15). If you diligently study the Word, you won't be ashamed when others ask you questions concerning the Bible and its meaning.

The Bible says we must *earnestly contend for the faith which was once delivered unto the saints* (Jude 1:3). That means we must apply ourselves, learn what God said, and let the Holy Ghost bring revelation.

Characteristics of the house of God

In studying how Jacob built a house of God, let me show you seven things about churches that we need to realize today:

1. The house of God is a place where sinners find mercy. Why do we even build a house of God? So sinners can find their way to Jesus. God proclaimed to Moses that He was *The Lord God, merciful and gracious, longsuffering, and abundant in goodness and truth, keeping mercy for thousands, forgiving iniquity and transgression and sin...* (Exodus 34:6,7). God also told Moses, *...I the Lord thy God am a jealous God, visiting the iniquity of the fathers upon the children unto the third and fourth generation of them that hate me; and showing mercy unto thousands of them that love me, and keep my commandments* (Exodus 20:5,6). Thank God, there can be a thousand generations of churches, and each one of them will be remembered as a house of mercy!

Jacob was a man on the run from God and from his enemies. He ran from his brother, Esau, from whom he had stolen the birthright of elder-son status and thus, the double-portion inheritance. Jacob had a track record of unrighteousness, but God interrupted that one night in the middle of the desert, when Jacob dreamed of a ladder where angels of God ascended and descended (see Genesis 28:12). After that night vision, Jacob was never the same. He had been apprehended by God and shown a better way to live. God interrupted his unrighteousness and changed his nature to righteousness.

There are men and women today who are being raised up by God to interrupt unrighteousness. The church has a voice, and that voice is the name of Jesus. When we use that name, everything we do and say is anointed. When we lay hands on the sick in that name, there is healing. When we cast out devils in that name, they flee. God has made us His peculiar vessels, and He has a way of taking us into every segment of the world. He wants to bring sinners out of sin and darkness into the light, in houses of mercy.

2. The church is the place where heaven is real. Why does God want us to prosper? He wants us to prosper so we'll build a haven on earth where the saints abide, and where there is a revelation of heaven on earth. John the Apostle saw the heavenly city descending to earth in a vision (see Revelation 21:2), and every man and women today needs to get that same revelation. Heaven is our eternal home and our reward, and we need to teach that truth.

Jacob received a revelation of heaven the night he dreamed of the ladder and the angels. Heaven is our real paycheck when this earthly life is over, not the money we make while we're here. But some people don't even realize what it is they're working for. They've never heard of those heavenly mansions or streets of gold, the gates of pearl, or the beautiful foundations set with precious stones of the heavenly city awaiting all saints...forever (see Revelation 21:10-21).

The church is the place where heaven is real and where people will get a little glimpse of it now and then.

3. The church is the place where God speaks to man with revelation knowledge. It's where God reveals himself to man—where He reveals His ways...heaven's way. That's what Jacob saw that night—something bigger than his natural man could comprehend...a vision so powerful that he could only understand it in spiritual terms. He could see that heaven had opened up to him, and as a result, he was forever changed. God doesn't want us to rely on our carnal minds for understanding— He wants us to have spiritual understanding...and the church is a good place to get it. The church is where we get a new spirit, where we renew our minds in the Word, and where we grow and develop from carnal to spiritual men and women.

4. The house of God is the place where angels reside. The Bible says the church is where angels are present. Hebrews 1:14 calls them *ministering spirits*. Angels are present at the gates of heaven. According to the Book of Psalms, angels respond to the sound of God's Word and to the sound of God's voice in His Word. So if we will just speak God's Word, angels in the spirit realm will become activated to minister to our needs.

5. The house of God is the place God gives to man. This is the place where God deposits ministry of the Word into the lives of people. It's a place where God imparts things to us. We serve a God who is the Alpha and Omega—the Beginning and the End. He is the First and also the Last (see Revelation 1:11, 21:6), and there is no end to Him whatsoever. He just keeps on blessing us, and He imparts the blessings in the house of God.

6. The house of God is the place where God and man join hands financially. Jacob received the revelation of who Jesus was when he covenanted with God to take him back to the place of safety, saying, "I will surely give a tenth of everything I have" (see Genesis 28:22). So the house of God is where God and man partner financially to fund the move of God on earth. Let the world fund the world...but let the church fund the church. God has blessed men and women and caused them to be raised up with millions—even billions—of dollars, and they are taking that money and putting it not in the world's system, but in the house of God so that the latter house truly will be greater than the former house (see Haggai 2:9). We must fund the house of God and move in the flow of the Holy Spirit.

7. The house of God is the place where the law of increase begins in our lives. There are spiritual laws of increase that are carefully laid out in the Bible, and the house of God is the place where those laws are activated. Jacob vowed a vow, and said, *If God will be with me, and will keep me in this way that I go, and will give me bread to eat, and raiment to put on, so that I come again to my father's house in peace; then shall the Lord be my God* (Genesis 28:20,21). And from that moment on, when we read about Jacob, we read about the increase—because from that point forward, God blessed Jacob financially.

Giving releases the law of increase. As we give to God our tithes and offerings—and as they are blessed in the house of God—the law of increase is activated and we are prospered.

There are two things you will need to learn to operate in—the law of release and the law of increase. And the house of God is where you will learn about these laws and where they will be activated. Release...and increase!

The law of release says this: "What I give to God, I release to Him!" Therefore, you won't be thinking about all the things you could have bought with that money if you hadn't given it in the offering plate.

Release! Then God will faithfully send the increase.

A place of peace

The house of God is the place where we learn how to prosper. And to a great degree, that prosperity is proportionate to the amount of peace we experience in our minds. God desires that we prosper, even as our souls prosper. Our souls learn to prosper in the house of God.

It's sad, but statistics prove that one of the leading causes of divorce in today's society has to do with money—not how money is handled, but lack of money, or money shortages. Money problems are also a leading cause of deception. Remember, the Bible warns that the love of money is the root of all evil.

This is a crooked generation we're living in. Everything has become distorted, twisted, bent out of shape. This is the generation that so badly needs to hear the gospel—that Jesus died for their sins, that He loves them, that He is coming back soon. The world needs to know that Jesus lives. He was crucified to atone for the sins of mankind—your sins, my sins—but He is no longer dead. His resurrection set us free, and He is alive forevermore.

The Church must tell that Good News. Acts 2:40 says, *And with many other words did he testify and exhort, saying, Save yourselves from this untoward generation.* That word *untoward* literally means "twisted, warped, crooked, and distorted." Thank God, Jesus has not only saved us from hell, but He has also made it possible for us to save ourselves from this *untoward* generation. He straightens out our thinking. He straightens out our problems. He straightens out our lives. He brings us up higher, making it possible for us to live on the level of the Word of God. He makes it possible for us to extricate ourselves from the twisted culture we live in.

The way we do that is to get into a Holy Ghost-filled, Bible-believing church. We do that by associating ourselves with Holy Ghost-filled people. Rather than acting like the world, we act like Holy Ghost-filled men and women. And the more we sit under the Word of God—the more it falls on us like rain—the more it changes us. Second Corinthians 3:18 says *we...are changed into* [his] *image from glory to glory, even as by the Spirit of the Lord.* Thank God, He has made it possible for us to change! Thank God, He has made it possible for us to save ourselves from this untoward generation!

Acts 2:41 says, *Then they that gladly received his word were baptized: and the same day there were added unto them about three thousand souls.* I believe the glory of the latter house of God will outshine the former house. In this day—these end times—there will be more souls won to Christ than in any other generation. More souls will be won than on the day of Pentecost. More souls will be won in this final hour than in any other period of earth's history. I don't know exactly how God is going to accomplish that. I only know that He has called me and Cindy and the congregation of Abundant Life Christian Center to do our parts. And that we are gladly doing.

With this Great Commission comes an incredible financial responsibility. There is a tremendous economic demand that comes upon a church when world evangelism begins to take place. Nine years ago, when Abundant Life Christian Center started with just Cindy and myself and ten people, it was difficult to foresee a time when we would preach to a congregation of thousands each week...or that we would literally reach millions of others via television and satellite. Our gross annual income that first year was $45,000. Nine years later, God has chosen to send millions of dollars through Abundant Life Christian Center. God has done His part to bless us because we have done our part to be faithful to Him and to the vision He has entrusted to us.

When we are faithful to the vision God has entrusted to us, He will multiply everything concerning us. He will multiply our tithes and offerings back to us. He will multiply us with children and grandchildren. He will multiply our household goods and worldly goods. He will multiply our businesses and financial dealings. For those of us in full-time ministry, He will multiply the number of souls saved under our preaching. He will multiply how we minister and the facilities we use to accomplish what He has called us to do. And all of that multiplication takes place because we are faithful in service to God.

Faithful and steadfast

The apostles were faithful, steadfast servants. Godly fear and divine respect was theirs, but those qualities are missing in some people today. Acts 2:43-45 says, *And fear came upon every soul: and many wonders and signs were done by the apostles. And all that believed were together, and had all things common; and sold their possessions and goods, and parted them to all men, as every man had need.* Now, God did not command people to go and sell everything they had and impart that to others. But the early church did that. It seems that God had placed such an economic demand upon this early church that He graced the people to react in such a way that they would literally sell all they had and share the proceeds so the house of God could be built quickly. Then the gospel was taken to the entire known world.

The early Christians took care of one another. They had to. They were living in dangerous times, when preaching the gospel could easily mean imprisonment or death. The early Christians saw to it that these first ministers were prayed for and fed and watered and clothed and taken in when necessary. But it is clear that the communal aspect of Christianity was peculiar to the times and not something God would demand of us today. We don't have to sell everything we have and give the money to the church.

But it is apparent to me that if we are going to fulfill the vision God has entrusted to us, we're going to have to do certain things: We're going to have to evangelize our neighborhoods and go into all the nations of the world. We have to be willing to evangelize both our own immediate communities and the world at large.

Between now and the year 2000, I can only imagine how the hearts of men will fail them. This world is full of fear and anxiety. We Christians have been sheltered in many ways, but the world is full of fear and trembling. Never before have so many men, women, and children been in such need of a living, risen Savior. The devil has the world by the throat, and the only remedy for that is Jesus.

Christians are fortunate because we have been delivered from the world's system. But those who are currently dominated by it will continue to be harassed and harangued to the point that their hearts will actually fail them. Heart attacks are still the leading cause of death in this nation. And what is a heart attack? Nothing more than heart failure. The Bible said these days would come upon mankind (see Luke 21:26).

And then there is the violence. It's gotten so bad that drugs, killings, and murders are just routine. They are no longer the exception. Violent crimes like these are the rule, even in smaller communities and rural areas. No place is safe any longer from violent crime. In large cities like Dallas and Los Angeles and New York, these violent crimes take place even on the freeways, leaving a trail of innocent victims for whom there are no easy answers.

I tell you, it's wonderful to serve God, but the world knows only violence and turmoil. In the church, you'll find peace and safety—but in the world, only fear. So one of the places where the glory of God will be most readily observed is in the house of God. We'll actually be seeing the glory of God manifested to greater and greater degrees in the house of God in these last days.

The house of God will be the place to find the peace of God. And the peace you and I take out of there with us will be quite remarkable for the world to behold. It will make us stand out more and more remarkably.

While those in the world will be walking around engulfed with fear and turmoil, anxiety and torment, Christians will be walking in peace and tranquility. We'll be walking around with a little bit of "church" all over us—and the world is going to want that. They are going to need it in these last days, just to make it through.

If we are going to be a part of this end-time, final move of God, we're going to have to be willing to participate in these outpourings of the Holy Ghost. If we don't, we're going to miss it. We're going to have to be willing to move in the power of God, manifesting signs and wonders. We're going to have to have the God-kind of heart, the kind of heart for soulwinning that will dig deep down in our pockets to give to the work of world evangelism. We're going to have to have a heart of community and a heart of love, as we take the resources gathered into God's storehouse—the Church—and use them to reach the world with the Good News of Jesus Christ.

10
Power to Get Wealth

> *But thou shalt remember the Lord thy God: for it is he that giveth thee power to get wealth, that he may establish his covenant which he sware unto thy fathers, as it is this day.*
> —Deuteronomy 8:18

Why does God want us to prosper? The Number One reason is to win souls. Another reason is that He just loves us and wants to bless us with prosperity. Yet another reason is so we will build the house of God through our tithes and offerings. Deuteronomy 8:18 states that one reason God wants us to prosper is so He can "establish His covenant" in the earth.

In order for that to happen, Jesus first had to come to earth. Second, He had to raise up His Church. That's who *we* are today. We are the Church of Jesus Christ—*the ones appointed and anointed to take the gospel to all corners of the earth.*

Something as ambitious as that takes resources. Isn't it interesting that when the Apostle Paul began to go forth into the world to establish the church, he began to boldly write things like, ...*my God shall supply all your need according to his riches in glory by Christ Jesus* (Philippians 4:19). If this means what I believe it means—that God will supply all of Paul's (and yours, and my) needs on heaven's level—then this passage of Scripture had to mean that Paul had at his disposal more than enough resources to build God's New Testament church. God gave Him power to get wealth so he could take the gospel to the nations that existed on earth in the period of time shortly after the Resurrection. And Paul accomplished his goal, which was also his earthly destiny.

Remember, God did not say He would give His people power to get wealth so they could sit back and coast, or get greedy and spend everything they have on themselves. He did not say He would give His people power to get wealth to turn them into rich "fat cats." No, He said He would give His people power to get wealth in order to establish His covenant.

And that's good news! In fact, that's powerful! God wants His covenant established on earth, and He's going to give us power to get wealth in order to accomplish that!

The glorious last days

As I have already stated, I believe we are living in the last days—that brief period of time just prior to the Rapture, when the Lord snatches up His Church to be with Him in heaven. He's coming back soon, and before that happens, He's going to rapture us out of here. But even before that happens, God is going to raise up men and women who will powerfully preach the gospel to all the world.

I believe it is accurate to say that we are living in the first generation that is capable of actually doing that. Technology has virtually exploded, giving us the means and the opportunity to take the gospel message to huge segments of the world's population—which is larger now than ever before—almost simultaneously. Via television satellite, short wave radio, and through large preaching ministries that are being raised up to address the masses anywhere there's room enough for a megacrowd, the gospel is going forth throughout the earth as never before.

In addition, there are more tongue-talking, Holy Ghost-filled, demon-chasing people on the planet than ever before who share the same vision to evangelize earth before the return of Jesus. We have the technology. We have the numbers. We have the means of travel that is unprecedented in the history of humanity. We have the knowledge of how to translate the Bible into virtually every known language that exists. We can reach practically the entire globe in just one telecast.

Politically, we are in position to go forth and preach powerfully because we can go through doors that were previously closed to the gospel. This is actually the first time in the history of the world that so many political walls have fallen down that Christians can go almost anywhere and preach. We are that generation predestined by God to take the gospel into all the world, and I say we must not run from the call. *We must answer it!*

And because there are more tongue-talking, Spirit-filled Christians living today than in Paul's generation, there is more money available in the body of Christ to support this great end-time evangelistic move of God. The fact that there is more money in the body of Christ today is not by accident—it is according to the perfect plan of God.

But consider this: The Word says, *Beloved, I wish above all things that thou mayest prosper and be in health, even as thy soul prospereth* (3 John 1:2). God's plan to prosper us is a total package that includes both mental and physical health. It would be a shame to have the power to get wealth, but to be too sick and infirm to do anything important for God with it. Therefore, that person on earth who has both the power to get wealth and the health to carry out the instructions of the Holy Ghost is indeed a mighty force to be reckoned with.

No more "just get by" theology

God's financial plan for His people today involves a whole lot more than "just getting by," as the Israelites did while they were in Egypt. They lived on a simple, poor diet of leeks and garlic and barley—and many of them didn't have enough to eat, so they died of starvation. The Israelites were living in poverty—just getting by, with a slave mentality—when God delivered them out of Egypt. When they finally listened to Moses, he led the Israelites out of Egypt...and straight into the wilderness.

Now, many people think the wilderness is a land of lack, but if you'll study those verses about the Israelites' journey through the wilderness in the Book of Exodus, you'll see that the people always had enough during their forty years of following the cloud by day and the pillar of fire by night.

In the mornings, they gathered manna that had fallen from heaven during the night. There was always just enough to get them through the day, but since the manna wouldn't keep overnight, each day the Israelites had to gather it anew. For a distraction from the steady diet of just manna, God sent quail. Just enough. And their clothes and shoes were just enough, since they didn't wear out for forty long years—a supernatural move of God to provide for His children. But God was calling the Israelites out from under that "just enough" mentality and into the land of "more than enough"—Cana, where there flowed milk and honey.

I personally dispute the mentality on earth today that confesses, "Lord, just give me enough to get by today!" That is not scriptural for the dispensation we are currently in. Nevertheless, that's the way some people still pray: "God, just get me by—give me enough to pay my bills, and I'll be happy!" To these people, I say, "You'd better change that kind of prayer. That is not New Testament prayer. That's old covenant prayer."

God does not want to give His people just enough, because He is Jehovah Jireh—the God who is more than enough. Two thousand years ago, when He arose from the dead and ascended to heaven to assume His seat at the right hand of the Father, Jesus activated that "more than enough" move of God. And God has not raised us up to that level only to send us back into the wilderness to "just get by."

We get what we ask for

Christians pray some of the silliest prayers on earth. Because of their unbelief, because of bad teaching, because of a religious spirit, they pray prayers to "just get by," when they could be praying bold prayers that produce abundance in their lives.

You've said it with your mouth fifteen-jillion times: "I hate living from paycheck to paycheck!" Yet it's still going on. Why is that? Because God answered your prayer: He gave you just enough. How many of those "just enough" prayers have you been praying without realizing it? How many times have you asked, "Lord, I just want another pair of shoes. Will You help me?" And so you got just that—one pair of shoes. There—you just got by for another little spell until you need another pair of shoes. Then when you need another pair, you'll do it again, and get just that—one more pair of shoes.

Or how about, "I wish that car would work!"—when what you really need is a brand-new car! Every time you turn around, you're asking God for something to just get by, instead of releasing your faith, standing on the Word, and asking God for more than enough! If you ask for just enough, that's exactly what you'll get!

But I am convinced that this is not the will of God for your life. You won't find "just getting by" in the New Testament church. Jesus shed His blood to overcome the "just get by" mentality in us. That same resurrection power is available to us in the financial realm. Jesus wants to do—and is capable of doing—so much more in your life in this hour. He wants you to have more than enough so you will give more than enough...and do your part to help finance the end-time evangelization of earth.

Now, I'm not belittling anybody who has it tough in life, because there are certainly people who have it tough. But Jesus can set people free from that, if they will just ask Him to get involved in their circumstances. He has more than enough to meet their needs.

So here were the Israelites, struggling along in the wilderness, just getting by. And they got out there so far that they sinned against God. So God killed every one of them and sent a whole new generation into the Promised Land.

A place of preparation, not lack

You see, the wilderness was not a land of lack but of preparation and training to ready the Israelites for the Promised Land. Deuteronomy 8:16-18 says, God *fed thee in the wilderness with manna, which thy fathers knew not, that he might humble thee, and that he might prove thee, to do thee good at thy latter end; And thou say in thine heart, My power and the might of mine hand hath gotten me this wealth. But thou shalt remember the Lord thy God: for it is he that giveth thee power to get wealth....*

God was saying, in these verses, "I'm going to send you out into the wilderness with just enough, to see if you will be faithful so I can trust you with more. All your life, you've been trying to just get by or just get a little more. But I'm calling you out from under that mentality of lack." So He purified His people and humbled them during that long wilderness experience.

After Moses died, Joshua became the leader of the Israelites. He was the right man for the job, since he was one of only two of the twelve men sent by Moses to spy out the Promised Land who came back with a good report. While the others lamented about fierce-looking giants in the land of plenty, Joshua and Caleb boldly said, "We are well able to take the land!"

Consequently, a trek through the wilderness that should have lasted just a few days was extended by God into forty years of weary wandering because the majority of the tribes of Israel were walking in unbelief. Here were men who had been set apart unto the service of the Lord, acting like cry-babies when it came time to go across Jordan and take the land that had been promised to them.

When the tribes came out of Egypt, the Lord directed Moses to circumcise all the men of Israel. That literally meant they were sanctified and set apart to do the work of God. But they did not follow through with that, so as they bore children and circumcised them according to the Lord's command, the children—not the parents—entered the Promised Land. All the original generation, with the exception of Joshua and Caleb, did not enter in. Only their offspring entered in.

Jericho taken by God's "youth group"

Now, forty years later, the army of Israel was reduced to a "youth group." They camped in a place called Gilgal—in

Hebrew, meaning "circle, sphere, unending." This is a type of the Word of God and its unending source as the answer for every problem there is or ever was or yet will be. For every problem, there is a solution in the Word of God.

As one of his first assignments from God, Joshua was ordered to take Jericho with these young, sanctified warriors. *And the Lord said unto Joshua, See, I have given into thine hand Jericho, and the king thereof, and the mighty men of valour* (Joshua 6:2). Now, *Jericho* is an interesting word that in Hebrew means "to smell, to anticipate, to enjoy." The Israelites could smell it, anticipate taking it, anticipate running the inhabitants out and having this magnificent city for themselves. And Jericho was shut up tight to the Israelites. Here was this city that had seemed impenetrable to the young Israelite warriors, but God was saying to Joshua, "I have given Jericho into your hand...."

What was it going to be? How could a bunch of overzealous teenagers scale the walls of a city like that? Yet these kids were fresh out of the wilderness, where they had been taught, "Some day we're going over to Cana," and they couldn't wait to move. They were tired of just smelling, anticipating the taste of freedom—they wanted to experience it for themselves.

So they believed God, followed Joshua, and got their marching orders directly from heaven. In a dramatic tale of victory over the seemingly impossible, Joshua led his army—preceded by a band of musicians—in a march around the walls of Jericho. And at the precise moment the horns were blown, the walls fell down (see verses 3-20)...and the rest is history.

The day faith comes

The greatest day in your life is when faith comes and you begin to see that what God said to Joshua is true for you also: "See, I have given into your hands Jericho...." Everything God does is by faith. So the greatest day in your life is when you begin to see what He has already done for you in the heavenly realm, and you begin to appropriate that spiritual reality into the natural realm, by faith.

You see, God is a faith God. The only way you can possibly please Him is by faith. Everything God ever did, He did by faith. And when you finally see with your spiritual eyes what you want to take place in the natural, it won't be long until you see it manifest in the natural realm in such a way that you can see it with your natural eyes.

If you can see it through eyes of faith, it won't be long until you'll be able to see with your natural eyes what God has said. He said He wants you to have Jericho—more than enough. A lot of times, what we see by faith in the spiritual realm is already done. God has already done it, but if you can't see it, you can't have it. On the other hand, if you *can* see it, you *can* have it!

But first you may have to conquer your own "Jericho."

He has given you the city

I believe God said to Joshua, "I have given Jericho into your hand—can you see it?" And I believe Joshua answered, "Yes, I see it!" Before Joshua could lead his people into the land of Cana, Jericho first had to be defeated.

The land of milk and honey—where there was more than enough for all—was just across the wall. Only the walls of Jericho separated Joshua and his people from prosperity that was beyond anything they had ever experienced. Across the wall was an end to the "just get by" mentality. Across the wall was abundance. And that's what God wants for His people today. He wants us to have more than enough—and like Joshua, we receive it through obedience.

The walls fall down

Jericho had huge walls, and those walls were made of great stone embarkments. Historians tell us that the walls were so thick that five or six chariots could be driven abreast on top of those walls and still have room to pass each other. The walls of Jericho were so massive that even the most uninformed onlooker could see how impenetrable they obviously were. To compound matters, inside there were giants. And a giant army. This border fortress city guarded the entrance to the land of Cana, and unless the Israelites could get past Jericho, they would never enter Cana.

But God had a strategy ready, and He told it to Joshua. It was Joshua's obedience to God's strategy that collapsed those massive walls. God said, *And ye shall compass the city, all ye men of war, and go round about the city once. Thus shalt thou do six days. And seven priests shall bear before the ark seven trumpets of rams' horns: and the seventh day ye shall compass the city seven times, and the priests shall blow with the trumpets* (Joshua 6:3,4). God told Joshua, "Get your army and your priests out there and march around the city because when I say so, the walls are going to fall!" Joshua and his men obeyed God to the letter, and as a result, they entered into abundance.

Now, God could have caused those walls to fall on day one, but He didn't do it that way. For seven days, those young Israelites who were scrapping for a fight had to walk passively and obediently around those thick buttresses, aching to swing a punch, toss a spear, or wield a sword. But obediently, they marched passively as the shofars sounded. Only on the seventh day did anything significant happen—and when it did, God got the complete glory as the impressive walls of Jericho fell down flat.

Those young men must have felt pretty silly, marching around the walls of mighty Jericho to the tune of trumpet music...probably feeling a little like pantywaists. I'll bet they had to confront every fear and insecurity imaginable. But when those feelings rose up in them, they just walked right around them and kept on going. That's what we must do today when fear rises up and says, "What if I can't pay the bills? What if I don't have enough money to just get by?" Like the Israelite army, we've got to train ourselves to walk around that stuff and keep right on going, until the walls of our own individual "Jericho" fall down and we walk over to the other side...into abundance, which is always the direct result of our obedience.

Today is the day to enter Jericho

I tell you, the first thing you need to say when you get up in the morning is, "Hello, Devil! My feet are on the planet again, and you're *under* my feet. I'm back, and here I go walking, in the name of Jesus, around every fear, every doubt, every problem, every symptom, every hint of unbelief." Then just open the Word of God and go right up to Gilgal. Encircle everything in the Word, then take Jericho by storm!

Some people live their whole lives dreaming of what they really want to do, but they never accomplish anything but dreaming. Don't let that happen to you. Today is the day you must do something about making that dream you've held in your heart become reality! Today is the day to take your "Jericho!"

Today is the day to enter Jericho, where there is more than enough for you. But how do you enter in? By the same kind of obedience that Joshua practiced as he marched around those walls and gave the order for the priests to blow those strange-looking trumpets. Abundance is separated from you by a wall of obedience. If you can get those walls to come down, you can have abundance.

Prime the pump

I'm reminded of a song I once heard about a man who was crossing the desert on foot. He was dying for a drink of water, and after a while, he came to an old pump—right there in the middle of the desert. So he grabbed the handle and tried it, only to discover that it was one of those old pumps that had to be primed with water in order to get it going. But right next to it, there was a bottle with a note on it that said, "Pour this water in the pump to prime it."

This guy picked up the bottle and stared at it longingly, thinking, *What if I pour this water into the pump and it doesn't work? Then I've just poured away my water, when I'm dying of thirst! But what if I drink it?* He thought about the alternatives for a while, then decided to pour the water into the pump. Sure enough, water flowed everywhere. There was plenty to drink, and plenty left over.

Deciding to obey God with our tithes and offerings is like that. If we give it away, we prime the pump of heaven. But if we keep it—if we drink it—it's gone forever and produces nothing into our lives.

So go ahead—prime the pump of heaven with the Holy Ghost. See how God will pour out abundance into your life because of your obedience.

Then there is the principle of consequences for those who choose to "drink it." Achan was ordered by God to go into the enemy's camp and destroy everything. He was specifically told not to take anything out of the camp with him. But here was this little wedge of gold, winking up at him—just a little one. Who'd miss it? "No one," he reasoned. So he took it...and brought a curse onto the entire tribe through his disobedience (see Joshua 7).

The things devoted to God

Let's look for a moment at what Joshua 6:17 says: *And the city shall be accursed....* Then verses 18,19 say, *And ye, in any wise keep yourselves from the accursed thing, lest ye make yourselves accursed, when ye take of the accursed [devoted] thing, and make the camp of Israel a curse, and trouble it. But all the silver, and gold, and vessels of brass and iron, are consecrated unto the Lord: they shall come into the treasury of the Lord.*

I can just see the children of Israel, chomping at the bit to get inside Jericho and see for themselves the riches it contained. But then God tells them that those same contents were to be His entirely. They were the firstfruits—the tithe—of what was to come. For forty years, the Israelites had been anticipating this moment. Then they were unable to touch anything in the city for themselves. Can you imagine the temptation they must have experienced the day they entered Jericho? But they knew the Word of God, and obeyed. They knew that if they disobeyed, they would bring a curse upon themselves and upon the entire camp of Israel.

The firstfruits of our labors are devoted to God, and if we take them, we're cursed. We must take that first tenth of everything and give it to Him, obediently, again and again. Eventually, that giving will produce a crop in our lives that comes straight from heaven. God will put clothes on our backs, food on our tables, and shoes on our childrens' feet if we consecrate those firstfruits to Him.

Now, that's exactly what Joshua did. Jericho was the first of numerous cities that the Israelites had to conquer in order to take the Promised Land and make it their own. After those walls came down, Joshua could have gone into Jericho and set up camp, keeping everything for himself and his people. He could have enjoyed the spoils of war for himself. But he didn't do that. *He consecrated Jericho as the firstfruit offering of the Promised Land to God*, and all the silver and brass and gold in the city was heaped up into a treasury and given to God.

Again God ordered the Israelites to take with them nothing out of Jericho. Jericho was the firstfruit of the Israelites' conquest of the Promised Land, and the Lord wanted to keep it for himself—which was His right. In addition, it was the firstfruit of the peoples' increase. Jericho and its entire contents represented the tithe of the very great amount of wealth and resources that was about to come into the hands of the Israelite people.

I can just see the children of Israel, eyeing all that stuff after a simple diet of manna and quail in the wilderness. They'd heard about it, and now they were seeing it, but they couldn't touch any of it because it all belonged to God. But they had passed the test and could now enter into Cana, where there would be plenty for all.

Cana is a type of the New Covenant that we walk in today. Even when you enter into that land of abundance God has prepared for you, there will still be giants of unbelief and doubt—in addition to other obstacles—that you'll have to conquer before you can set up camp. For forty years, the Israelites were just at the edges of Cana, smelling its fragrance, dreaming about entering in. When they finally got there, it was such a temptation for those young men to take a little for themselves. But they were obedient and gave God what was rightfully His —the tithe.

Your own Promised Land

There's a lesson in this for you and me today. Keep the firstfruits of your labor, and you are cursed. Release it—give it to God—and you'll be blessed and increased. You can be assured that the walls of your own Jericho will fall down when you are obedient to God's laws regarding tithing and standing on the Word. The walls will fall down so you can enter into Cana and your own Promised Land—the land flowing with milk and honey.

God has a "Promised Land" for each of us. It's that place of more than enough. To get there, you will have to defy the criticism and the heckling, the doubt and unbelief, the obstacles and the seeming impossibilities. All these giants—and more— will leap out to frighten you and keep you from entering in. But God has a plan for you to step right around those obstacles and march according to His strategies until the walls of your own "Jericho" come tumbling down.

On the other side of those walls is more than enough. Abundance is there. Whether it happens on the first day, the second day, the third day, the seventh day, the twentieth day, or the twelfth year—God has a plan for you to enter into your own personal "Promised Land." Obedience is your key to getting there. However long it takes, if you'll just be obedient to God and take Him at His Word—if you'll just tithe and give out of a willing and obedient heart—you'll get there.

You will enter into that place of abundance God has prepared for you if you obey Him. You have a choice—to obey or not obey. Whether or not you enter into this land of abundance depends on the choice you make.

Blanketing the world with the gospel

I believe the next manifestation of Jesus Christ on earth will be the rapture of the Church. All things are ready for that to take place. I believe that before the Great Tribulation period begins, the Rapture will occur. Jesus will lift His Church out of here, but even before that takes place, He is raising up a generation of men and women who will turn the world upside down for Him. This generation—yours and mine—will do whatever it takes and pay whatever it costs to blanket the earth with the gospel. We are the ones who will preach powerfully to the people of this planet. Jesus said, *Go ye into all the world, and preach the gospel to every creature* (Mark 16:15). That was His Great Commission to us in His final moments on earth. We're the ones who are going to do it, and that is why we have been given the power to get wealth. It's what we're going to need to accomplish that Great Commission on the earth today.

We tongue-talking, demon-chasing, Bible-believing, power-preaching Holy Ghost men and women are the ones—more than any other Christians in history—who have the technology at our disposal to get the job done. We're the ones for whom it is possible to preach to every man, woman, and child on the planet. We can go through doors previously closed. We can take the gospel to the world via sophisticated telecommunications our grandparents never even dreamed would be invented. And we have access to all these avenues of preaching.

So we can easily see Deuteronomy 8:18 at work on the earth today: *...it is he that giveth thee power to get wealth, that he may establish his covenant....* He wants to prosper us, not so we'll become rich fat-cats, cozy in our velvet-lined pew, but so He can use us to get the Word out to the nations.

11
What to Do First When You Enter the Promised Land

Did you know that God has a Promised Land for you? The Promised Land is where abundance is...where there is no lack...where there is plenty for you and your family, with some left over...where your dreams are realized...where you are the most fruitful...where you receive the increase and where you learn to give to God with outrageous generosity. It's where you reside once you've learned that God's not broke—and neither are you!

The Promised Land is the place of faithfulness and supply. It's where you live once you've broken out of that "just get by" mentality and adopted the mentality of "more than enough."

And the first thing you do when you enter the Promised Land is what Joshua did: You tithe.

Here is what Deuteronomy 26 says you must do:

> *And it shall be, when thou art come in unto the land which the Lord thy God giveth thee for an inheritance, and possessest it, and dwellest therein; that thou shalt take of the first of all the fruit of the earth, which thou shalt bring of thy land that the Lord thy God giveth thee, and shalt put it in a basket, and shalt go unto the place which the Lord thy God shall choose to place his name there. And thou shalt go unto the priest that shall be in those days, and say unto him, I profess this day unto the Lord*

> *thy God, that I am come unto the country which the Lord sware unto our fathers for to give us. And the priest shall take the basket out of thine hand, and set it down before the altar of the Lord thy God. And thou shalt speak and say before the Lord thy God* [this was the confession of the children of Israel], *A Syrian ready to perish was my father, and he went down into Egypt, and sojourned there with a few, and became there a nation, great, mighty, and populous: And the Egyptians evil entreated us, and afflicted us, and laid upon us hard bondage: And when we cried unto the Lord God of our fathers, the Lord heard our voice, and looked on our affliction, and our labour, and our oppression: And the Lord brought us forth out of Egypt with a mighty hand, and with an outstretched arm, and with great terribleness, and with signs, and with wonders: And he hath brought us into this place, and hath given us this land, even a land that floweth with milk and honey.*
>
> *And now, behold, I have brought the firstfruits of the land, which thou, O Lord, hast given me. And thou shalt set it before the Lord thy God, and worship before the Lord thy God: And thou shalt rejoice in every good thing which the Lord thy God hath given unto thee, and unto thine house, thou, and the Levite, and the stranger that is among you* (vv.1-11).

Glory to God! It can't be made any plainer than that! You're to bring your tithe, set it before God, confess to Him that He is the One who brought you out of Egypt and into the land where there is milk and honey flowing. Then you're to worship Him with that tithe and rejoice in what He's done for you!

In so doing, you are "energizing" or "activating" the power of the Holy Ghost over your offering. Let me explain what I mean by that statement.

The Holy Ghost: God's Energy Source
The Holy Ghost is the energy source of heaven. The Holy Ghost is what came upon Jesus, as He was being baptized by John in the River Jordan (see Mark 1:10). Three-and-a-half years later, that same Spirit raised Him from the dead. The Scripture says the Holy Spirit "quickened His flesh" (see John 6:62,63). In other words, it energized His mortal body.

But the Holy Ghost—the Third Person in the Trinity—has been in existence as long as God has been in existence. When God created heaven and earth, *the Spirit of God moved upon the face of the waters* (Genesis 1:2). When the earth was full of darkness, the Holy Ghost "brooded over" it just as a mother hen broods over her eggs, keeping them warm until they're ready to hatch. In so doing, the Holy Ghost caused the water to warm—even in the absence of sunlight. It must have been mighty cold on planet earth until then—perhaps even frozen over, as the scientists declare. Only God knows what caused the earth's surface to be frozen—maybe it happened when Lucifer fell from heaven to earth with all of his rebellious angels. But the Holy Ghost "un-froze" it as He brooded over the earth, warming the frozen waters until all that ice melted.

Even before the sun and moon existed, the Holy Ghost existed and was operating on the face of planet earth. Heaven's Power Source!

Ephesians 1:19-21 states that the Holy Ghost demonstrated *the exceeding greatness of his power to us-ward who believe, according to the working of his mighty power, which he wrought in Christ, when he raised him from the dead, and set him at his own right hand in the heavenly places, far above all principality, and power, and might, and dominion, and every name that is named, not only in this world, but also in that which is to come.*

The word *wrought* is the Greek word for *activate*. It means "to flip" (like a switch) or "to turn on." So when God wrought Jesus from the dead, He activated—or turned on—heaven's resources to the Church. It's like having one great big breaker-box, one huge power source coming into the Church, with all these little breakers hooked up to that one big circuit. Jesus is the Main Breaker, and you and I are the little breakers, plugged into that main breaker-box. When the Holy Ghost turned Jesus on—Boom! Power shot through heaven, and down to earth where we are! To every person who believes, that power is available. When you were born again, that heavenly power became available to you. God energized you on the inside, and His Spirit came to reside inside you. At that moment, you became a living soul, made in the likeness and the image of God.

And so the Holy Ghost energizes God's Word. I am convinced that the same works Jesus did, we can do on earth—and even greater works (see John 14:12).

Now that you have entered in

I believe that once you have entered in to this personal "Promised Land," you should find the place where God has chosen to place His name, and where you know in your spirit God wants you to learn and to receive from Him. By that, I mean you must make sure you are attending the church God intends for you to be in. He has a place for you to give and receive and learn and grow. Are you where He intends for you to be?

I believe God calls the people who attend Abundant Life Christian Center to come here and be a part of our worldwide outreach. The people of this flock share that calling of world evangelism, and each person takes very seriously the work they have been called to do on earth until the Lord returns.

Can you say the same thing? Do you know for certain that the place where you worship is where God would have you remain? That's something you must get settled in your spirit, now that you have entered into the Promised Land. If you know you're called to be right where you are, then by all means, stay put. But if you can't say that for certain, it's time to pray and seek God for His direction.

The Word says God chooses the place where He will put His name. That means if He didn't choose the place you're in, you shouldn't be there. The church where you attend may be a good work, but it also may be one that was begun by a man or woman with good intentions...and not the Holy Spirit. You want to be where the Holy Spirit is. I've been in churches that were deader than six funeral homes. And, believe me, you don't want that! You want to be where there is life. Abundant life!

So be open for the Holy Ghost to move you to a place where there is life in the Spirit—a place where you'll learn and grow and perform great works for God, now that you have entered in.

Then, when you have been prospered and have put your firstfruits and your gifts into the bucket, you can know for certain that what you just gave is going to expand the work of God on earth in these last days. I didn't write this—God did. He said it, not me. This is not the gospel according to Walter. This is the Great Commission: *Go ye into all the world, and preach the gospel to every creature* (Mark 16:15).

I want you to get to the place where you have vision for that...so it will motivate your giving. You need to give because you want to—not because you have to. No one has to give. If you come to my church and don't give, I won't kick you out. You won't give until God deals with your heart to give, but even then you may give out of something other than generosity. But when you get the vision to give for soulwinning, you'll find the motivation to give generously—and when you get there, you'll be free.

According to the Word, there are reasons why people don't honor God by giving their tithes and offerings. Perhaps they don't fully understand what God has brought them out of. Perhaps it's due to some false way of thinking. Maybe it's because of pride that they refuse to admit what God has done for them. But if they'll just keep coming to church, they'll eventually get rhema about giving and get free of that stuff that's keeping them from giving out of the correct spirit and for the right reasons.

You see, there are only three rituals that followed believers from the old covenant into the new covenant—and all of these are done by faith.

The first is **anointing with oil**. We anoint people with oil, in the name of Jesus, and we anoint them by faith. Any kind of oil will do. What makes it holy is our obedience to God in doing it, and the faith that is released as we perform this old-covenant ritual. Without faith, it's impossible to get heaven's cooperation. But when we anoint with oil, by faith, everything is possible to him who believes.

The second is **water baptism**. This is a very powerful old-covenant ritual, and it alone won't save you. But it does signify bringing forth something new from the old. We do it to enter in to the born-again lifestyle, free of the bondage of sin and the former sinful life. We put it to death and bury it at the bottom of the baptismal pool.

The third is the **ritual of communion**. This is very powerful in itself, signifying the death and resurrection of our Lord. Again, we are not saved by it, but we are brought to inward examination of our lives of faith and motives of heart as we eat the bread—His body—and drink the wine—His blood. It is something we enter in to by faith, reverently, on the level of the Word of God.

But there is a fourth ritual that has followed the believer from the old to the new covenant, and that is the ritual of **tithes and offerings**.

Deuteronomy 26:4 says, *The priest shall take the basket out of thine hand, and set it down before the altar of the Lord thy God. And thou shalt speak and say before the Lord thy God, A Syrian ready to perish was my father....* And that's what we must do today: We must put our tithes and offerings into the basket, lay it on the altar of God, and then say, "Here it is, Lord. You alone are the One who has blessed me. You alone have brought me to this Promised Land. Jesus, You are the sacrifice, and You are the altar. I'm totally Yours—lock, stock, and barrel—from this time forward. So I come to You today, by faith, and I lay down my life before You. I'm laying everything I have on the altar of God. You are the One who has blessed me and brought me into this good land, and I will serve You here with everything I am and with everything I have. Thank You, Lord, for what You have given to me this week. Here is Your portion, and here is my offering."

And in so doing, you are entering into a powerful covenant with God, in which He promises to bless you. You are literally laying your gift on the altar of God as your part in the agreement. God's part of the agreement is to bless you and multiply you and make you prosperous.

Who was the Syrian?

Some biblical scholars believe the "Syrian" mentioned in verse five was Abraham. That may be, but I also believe this simply typifies a person bound for hell, short of the mercy and grace of God. We're all that way until we're born again and filled with the Holy Spirit. Then mercy swoops down in the Person of Jesus Christ, saves us, gives us revelation of eternity, changes our lives, and suddenly we see that it was God who brought us out of the land of perishing. It was God who brought us out of that place where we were being destroyed. He brought us out, and set our feet on solid ground, in a place that was large and blessed and filled with abundance to more than meet our needs.

Giving your gifts and tithes on the altar of God is a very powerful thing because you are actually saying, "Lord, You have delivered me from my yesterdays. My yesterdays were dark and getting darker. Then You changed my life. Now, as I bring these firstfruits to You, I just want to say thank You, because I was a Syrian—ready to perish—and You interrupted the path I was on. That path led to death, but the path You have put me on leads to eternal life. Thank You, God, that I did not choose You, but You chose me and ordained me to serve You the rest of my days."

Lay your gift at the altar of God and pray over it. That prayer of blessing energizes your giving and you'll receive a revelation regarding giving that will virtually change your life.

You'll become eager—willing—to give generously, even hilariously to God.

As you give to God, it's your way of saying, "Lord, You have taken me out from where I was, and You have changed my life. You have established my goings. You have saved me and sanctified me. You have taken me out of the path of poverty, death, disease, and hard bondage, and You have turned my life around. I am no longer in bondage. I am in Egypt no longer. I am no longer a Syrian slave, bound to perish. Today I am a child of the Most High God. I am a member of the household of faith. I am a citizen of heaven." That's powerful! That will activate all of heaven on your behalf, and the blessings will begin to fall!

The Holy Ghost will cooperate with your giving, if you give out of a correct understanding of what it means to lay your gift on the altar of God. You do it by obedience. You do it by faith. You do it with the intent of honoring and worshiping God for all He has done for you. Your offering then becomes a culmination of all the goodness God has shown to you. You don't just peel off fourteen dollars and toss it into the offering plate. You give carefully, with the intent of worshiping God and honoring His goodness to you. Then see what happens as your gift is activated—energized by the Holy Ghost. The blessings will start to rise up and overtake you, just as God promised in Deuteronomy 28:2.

Exactly when that happens is hard to chart, however, since as you pray, things begin to compound in God's economy. Your praying births things in the Spirit, and those things begin to come to pass according to the plan of God in your life. Things begin to link together, much as the thread of faith that winds throughout the Bible, from the Book of Genesis right through to the end of the Book of Revelation. You start to see the common thread of Jesus, according to the anointing, weaving together the events of your life into one beautiful tapestry. So it's not a matter of being able to see exactly when prosperity happened. It's more a matter of stepping back to see the entire picture as it began to develop, from the moment you began to serve God, obey Him, and present your tithes and offerings. It's when you stopped making all those dumb mistakes. It's when you started getting the big breaks, the best accounts. That's when deliverance hit your life.

As you lay your gift on the altar of God and pray over it to activate it by the Holy Ghost, you are recalling all these many blessings and saying, "Thank You, God! Thank You so much for what You have done for me!" And heaven hears that, and great things are released into your life spiritually.

Deuteronomy 26:9 states: *And he hath brought us into this place, and hath given us this land, even a land that floweth with milk and honey.* Don't ever forget the fact that God has brought you into every blessing you currently experience in life. *Every good gift and every perfect gift is from above, and cometh down from the Father of lights, with whom is no variableness, neither shadow of turning* (James 1:17). He is faithful to bless you as you give. So if there is an area of need in your life, there are some tremendous blessings prepared for you that are on the way. Rejoice—because the blessings are on the way!

Isn't it interesting that the firstfruits of your labor belong to God, and that this is exactly what the devil tries to prevent you from giving? The devil puts pressure on everyone to keep them from giving to God out of obedience and a willing heart. Every person, from Abraham forward, has had to resist the devil on this one front. Abraham fought the devil off his offering and prevailed. That's why he's listed in the Book of Hebrews as a man of faith. When the King of Sodom came to him to try to talk him out of giving his tithe to God, Abraham stood fast and was found faithful (see Genesis 14). That's why God said his faith was imputed to him—credited to him—as righteousness (see Romans 4). When you give to God after the manner of Abraham, your faith is imputed to you as righteousness. You are performing an act of faith. In fact, it's one of the highest forms of faith that you will ever operate in. It's a high form of worship because you are bringing your firstfruits before

God, laying them upon the altar, and worshiping the Lord with what you have.

Don't forget God!
Now, when you arrive in the Promised Land, don't forget the God who brought you there. *For the Lord thy God bringeth thee into a good land, a land of brooks of water, of fountains and depths that spring out of valleys and hills; a land of wheat, and barley, and vines, and fig trees, and pomegranates; a land of oil olive, and honey; a land wherein thou shalt eat bread without scarceness, thou shalt not lack any thing in it; a land whose stones are iron, and out of whose hills thou mayest dig brass* (Deuteronomy 8:7-9). The Hebrew word for *brass* is interesting in that it is the same word as for copper. In other words, precious metals will be mined there in the hills.

Verse 10: *When thou hast eaten and art full, then thou shalt bless the Lord thy God for the good land which he hath given thee.* Thank God, He is a good God! Thank God, He is a giving God! He does not want to take from you. He wants to *give* to you!

Beware that thou forget not the Lord thy God...lest when thou hast eaten and art full, and hast built goodly houses, and dwelt therein; and when thy herds and thy flocks multiply, and thy silver and thy gold is multiplied, and all that thou hast is multiplied; then thine heart be lifted up, and thou forget the Lord thy God (vv.11-14).

It happens. I'm sorry to have to say it, but it happens. People pray and fast and finally enter the Promised Land, where there is no lack—where there is more than enough of everything—and then they forget how they got there. They forget God. They begin to take the credit for getting themselves there. They stop tithing. They stop giving. They stop speaking correctly about the Lord and all He has done for them.

I can't tell you how many times people have come to me and said, "Pastor! I'm in urgent need of a job! Please pray for me!" So we would pray together, and they would get the job they so desperately needed. But when they get it, do they tithe?

Do they pay their bills? Do they provide for their household? Do they give offerings faithfully? Are they a good employee? Do they show up on time? Do they curse their employer behind his back?

If God gives you something—including a job—it is a blessing, not a curse, and it should be treated with respect and regarded as a blessing from God. When it is not appreciated—when God is forgotten—those same blessings may be lost.

Then here come these same people back to church (they may not have been there since they got that fabulous job), back to the altar, requesting prayer. "Pastor, I lost that job and I'm desperate. I repent! I repent! Please pray!"

"Sure," I say. "We'll pray that you'll get another job. But I don't want you to be so blessed that you can't serve God! This time, don't forget Who is trying to bring you out of those problems. It's God blessing you. Don't forget Him!"

I recall a story I heard years ago about a man who promised a preacher that he would give twenty percent of everything he made if God would just bless his business. So the two men prayed, and God began to bless this man's business to the point that at one time, he was writing checks in the amount of $20,000 a month. When the amount grew to $50,000 a month, he came back to the preacher and asked to be released from his oath. He said, "Pastor, please release me. I just can't afford it. Will you pray with me?" So the pastor prayed, "Lord, please cut this man's business back to the level where he can continue to obey You."

I'm sure this prayer was not the one the man expected to be prayed, but the idea is this—obeying God, serving Him, remembering Him as the Author of all our blessings is more important than any amount of money we could possibly make. And when those blessings begin to flow, there will be serious pressure applied to get our eyes off God.

See that your heart is not lifted up. Don't get to the place where you are so blessed that you can't give God what is rightfully His. You see, God will bless you to the degree that He can trust you. In Deuteronomy 8:16, He reminded the Israelites that

He was the One *who fed thee in the wilderness with manna, which thy fathers knew not, that he might humble thee, and that he might prove thee, to do thee good at thy latter end.*

God has always wanted to bless you. That was always His intent. Going through that wilderness, giving you just enough to get by, was simply a test to prove whether or not you would be faithful in the Promised Land. So you're there. Now what?

Give in faith

Many of the Israelites were never allowed to cross over Jordan into Cana. They were not allowed to cross over because God knew they would not be faithful once they got there. Only Joshua and Caleb had proven their faithfulness, and they were the only two of the older generation who were allowed to enter the Promised Land.

Imagine how surprised the others were—those who had heard story after story of the wonderful things to be found in the Promised Land—to learn they would never be allowed to go there themselves. This great land—the land that flowed with milk and honey, the land where there was plenty of gold and silver and where copper could be mined from the hills—was marked "off limits" to those unbelieving Israelites who had doubted and murmured their way through the wilderness experience.

Those who did enter, crossed the Jordan and immediately came upon Jericho—a forbidding city of foreboding walls. Nevertheless, it was a sweet-smelling place that promised blessings on the other side of those thick stone walls. What did they do the minute they conquered Jericho? Those Israelites took it before God and offered the whole city and all its contents before God, as a tithe for what was sure to come. They had anticipated taking that city. They had seen it from afar and smelled its sweet odors. But instead of keeping it for themselves, those Israelites whose hearts had already been proven faithful before God offered the entire city to the Lord as firstfruits of the Promised Land. In so doing, they humbled themselves before God, suppressed their own carnality, and defied all their fears. Then God said, "You can have all of Cana. Now you and your children will be blessed."

That is exactly what God is still doing with you and me. This principle of tithing and offering to God is not new, nor is it unique to this generation. Tithing is one of the ways God blesses households of today. He is looking for faithful men and women who will lead their families in righteousness. He is looking for faithful ones who will catch the vision for this thing and begin giving their tithes and offerings on the basis of what they actually earn each week, instead of tossing five or ten dollars in the offering plate when it comes around.

Are you afraid you can't do it on what you make? Yes, you can! Defy your fears! Overcome them! Then expect a fabulous return on that investment in God's kingdom—a return totaling a hundred, or sixty, or thirty times more than what you gave. That's what the Bible says, so believe it!

12
How to Turn It Around

So let's say you are familiar with what the Word says about tithing and giving offerings unto the Lord—but you aren't doing it. What now?

Isaiah 55:6,7 states: *Seek ye the Lord while he may be found, call ye upon him while he is near: Let the wicked forsake his way, and the unrighteous man his thoughts: and let him return unto the Lord....* Now, this scripture verse is not limited to the unbeliever. The believer who is currently in sin is also covered here. What now? Stop sinning! To withhold the tithe from God is to sin against Him. So today is the day to make the decision to stop that and to serve Jesus.

God wants to bless your life. He does not want anyone or anything to steal from you the many blessings Jesus acquired for you through His death, burial, and resurrection. And sin in your life can stop the glory of God from being manifested in you.

The Bible says, "Stop sinning!" *Let the wicked forsake his way....* Then verse 7 continues: *...let him return unto the Lord, and he will have mercy upon him; and to our God, for he will abundantly pardon.* It's so good to know that God will pardon every iniquity. He'll pardon every sin. He'll pardon every act of unrighteousness. If we'll just repent and return to the Lord, He's faithful to pardon us.

But it's important that we don't just repent out of a guilty conscience or from the motive I call, "I'm so sorry...because I got caught!" That's not true repentance! True repentance involves genuine sorrow over having committed the sin in the first place. True repentance mixed with godly sorrow will yield righteousness. It says so in the Word. Then you'll be able to stand before God and say, "Lord, I'm not repenting just because I'm sorry I got caught. I'm repenting because I'm turning my life over to You—including all those areas I've held back. I'm turning everything over to You, Lord, and I return to You."

Then He will abundantly pardon!

God's ways are higher

Verses 8,9 state: *For my thoughts are not your thoughts, neither are your ways my ways, saith the Lord. For as the heavens are higher than the earth, so are my ways higher than your ways, and my thoughts than your thoughts.* Notice that God makes a big distinction between His thoughts and His ways, and our thoughts and our ways. When Jesus of Nazareth comes into our lives, we need to move up to another level in order to live life as He wants us to live it. Now that we've been saved and filled with the Holy Spirit, we can no longer afford to think the way we did before we were saved. God is saying, "Come up higher! My thoughts and My ways are higher!"

For example, before I came up higher, I used to think life was about living for whatever I could get out of it. I call it the WIIFM mentality—"What's in it for me?" But that was then, and this is now—when I realize life is about the WIIFG mentality—"What's in it for God?" Now I realize that the WIIFM mentality is dangerous. That person may try to con you. That person may try to take advantage of you. That WIIFM person is someone you're going to have to watch.

Before I came up higher, I used to see a sick person and wonder, *How long is it going to be before they die?* Now, when I see a sick person, I say, "Hallelujah! There's a candidate for divine healing!" My thoughts have changed as a result of moving up to another level in God.

Our ways should be constantly changing. We should be constantly going higher in the ways of the Lord. We should be learning a different way of thinking, a different way of doing things.

Isaiah 55:10,11 gives this description of God's Word: *For as the rain cometh down, and the snow from heaven, and re-*

turneth not thither, but watereth the earth, and maketh it bring forth and bud, that it may give seed to the sower, and bread to the eater: So shall my word be that goeth forth out of my mouth. That's one of the most powerful passages in the entire Bible! In it, God describes His Word as heavenly "precipitation." It comes down from heaven, hits the earth, and literally automatically takes its course in nature. It causes whatever it falls upon to break forth and to bud. The earth doesn't have any option: It must obey the Word. It must bud. It must break forth.

The Bible calls the Word heavenly "rain." All life is sustained by water, and all that is required for each plant on earth to grow is that it be watered—one drop at a time. Think about it! California's giant Sequoia trees and giant redwoods, and every other massive plant upon this planet, all began as one individual seed that was watered by a single drop of water...and then another...and another...until a fully grown plant specimen finally emerged. Some of those trees are hundreds of years old now, and they're massive. They grow to be hundreds of feet high, and seventy-five to one hundred feet in diameter. They're so wide, you could drive tractor trailers side by side through the center of one of those trees and still have room to spare. They're awesome. Yet, no matter how large these trees grow, they still need water. They can't survive without it. Regardless of how massive they look on the outside, without water the trees cannot sustain life.

The water of the Word

By the same token, verse 10 states that the Word of God is like the rain that falls to earth—like drops of water. It goes forth from the mouth of God and accomplishes those very specific tasks God has assigned for it to perform.

Now, water is an interesting substance. It's crystal-clear, and when it falls to earth, it doesn't look like much. As it's falling, it looks like liquefied air. But that very crystal-clear substance contains every life-producing element that comes from the clouds. When it falls upon earth, rain has a delayed reaction. If there is a seed in the ground and the water falls upon it, that seed will begin to produce—but not immediately. The moment the water falls upon it, in the unseen realm, something begins to take place within that seed—slowly...one drop of water at a time. A chain reaction takes place beneath the earth, away from view. On the surface, nothing appears to be happening. But as more and more water falls upon that seed, the ground begins to break open, and a tiny shoot breaks forth. Then a sprout. Next, a miracle! The tiny likeness of a tree!

That little seed first began to germinate. Then it took root and grew beneath the surface of the earth. Then it budded and shot forth to the surface. And then it became a seedling and, finally, a tree. What appears to be dead may seem dry and barren, but just add water and everything begins to green up and change. Suddenly it's livable and can sustain life.

But verse ten is not about horticultural principles on planet earth. It's about the way the spirit-realm works. Every word that proceeds from the mouth of God has the potential to change your life. Your life may be bound up right now—locked up tight. It may be bound up in a dungeon of disease or depression. It may be shut up in a prison of poverty or prejudice. It may be bound up by every iniquity the devil has ever loosed upon planet earth. But I have good news! God did not leave us without the ability to restructure our society. He said, "I have a word that will rain on you—and when it does, it will begin to set you free! It will start way down in your spirit when it looks like nothing much is happening, and it will germinate there. Then it will begin to grow roots...shoot forth...and eventually become fully grown. When that happens, it will surely set you free!"

When the water of the Word hits your life, it will change your thinking processes. It's the Living Word, and when it begins to work inside your spirit-man, your ways will slowly become His higher ways. Slowly, something will begin to move inside you, and that rock of sickness or depression or poverty will move off you as the Word falls on you. You'll come to life where everything appeared to be dead and barren. The rain that falls out of heaven has a powerful ingredient in it—one that will sustain life. It has the Word of God in it—that life-producing force that is the very beginning of life on earth.

The components of the Word

The Word of God is made up of two components: *faith* and *desire*. We know that faith comes by hearing the Word (see Romans 10:17). Then a divine desire begins to grow on the inside of us. Another word for *desire* is *vision*. By faith, we begin to "see" the outcome. We catch the vision for what we conceive, by faith. The outcome cannot be produced, except by faith. But until the outcome is manifested, the desire—or the vision—for it springs up within us. Put there by God, that vision begins to produce God's thoughts and God's ways within us. And that vision sustains us until it's time for the crop to come in.

As the Word of God falls upon that seed within us, it is watered. Even though we can't yet see the manifestation of the outcome we desire, by faith we can envision it. We receive thoughts from God that are on an entirely new level because we are believing to receive.

A good example of this occurred on the day God called me to preach the gospel. There I was, one moment preparing to leave the house to hear a man preach at our church. The next, I was experiencing an open vision in which I saw myself doing the preaching. As I saw this taking place in my spirit, the Holy Ghost spoke to me. It was as if my entire surroundings had been blacked out momentarily. I didn't see masses of people. I didn't see pulpits or television cameras. All I could see was me ...and I was preaching. From that moment on, I was literally obsessed with just one thing: preaching the gospel. It was all I could think about, all that I wanted to do. I put my business up for sale and divested myself completely of everything else. I said to the Lord, "Whatever You want me to do, I'll do it. Wherever You want me to go, I'll go." I forsook my former ways when I got that one word from God. It took root and began to bud on the inside of me. And something happened.

I started to think different thoughts. I started to see people who were sick as healed. I started to see them getting well, in Jesus' name. I started to move in His ways. I read the Book of Acts, and began to lay hands on people and pray for them by the power of the Holy Ghost.

One day as I read Acts 19:20—*So mightily grew the word of God and prevailed*—the Holy Ghost spoke to me. He said, "You don't have any problems you can't overcome—you just outgrow them." That is powerful! I began to see that growing in the Lord was like growing a garden. If you want your garden to grow, you water it. It's the same with your spirit: If you want it to grow...water it! Water it well with the Word of God. The more water you put on it, the better it will grow.

The Holy Ghost continued to speak to me that day: "Any time you face a problem, Walter—any time you face opposition, any time you face any type of hindrance to the will of God in your life—you can outgrow that problem. Just put more water of the Word on it, and you'll find that "so mightily will grow the Word of God" in you, and you will prevail."

How to become great for God

You see, great men and women of God are not born great. They are just ordinary people who trusted in a big God, and who learned to outgrow every attack of the devil. They are little men and little women who consistently trust a big God and who water themselves with the Word until it prevails against each problem they face. Their thoughts become like God's thoughts. Their thoughts grow larger and larger, until they no longer have little thoughts. They have big, expansive thoughts—big enough to overcome any problem or hindrance facing them.

In this hour on earth, when the entire creation is groaning and travailing toward the day of Christ's return (see Romans 8:22), God is saying, "Let Me do with you as I did with Abraham. Let me raise up men and women out of you who will be known as priests and kings on the earth." And when you say "yes" to Him, you'll discover that your thoughts will begin to change and conform to His thoughts. Once the Holy Ghost gets ahold of you, you'll stop thinking of yourself as a victim of society. You're not the victim! You're the *victor!* The Word says you're an overcomer—that you have overcome Satan by the blood of the Lamb and the word of your testimony. Glory to God!

Isaiah 55:11 tells us more about the Word of God: *So shall my word be that goeth forth out of my mouth: it shall not return unto me void, but it shall accomplish that which I please, and it shall prosper in the thing whereto I sent it.*

How can you be a victim when the Word of God is out there in front of you, working on your behalf to produce fruit? You see, one translation of verse 11 is this: "My word will not return unto me unproductive or ineffective." Realize that when the Word of God goes forth, it has an effect. It makes an impact. When God's Word comes upon you, you stop feeding the problem with the way you talk and start praying in tongues. You stop confessing the worst and start believing God, by faith, for His best to come forth in your life. You stop worrying about your unsaved loved ones and start calling their names out before the Lord, believing Him for their salvation.

The wonderful Wesleys

One of the most moving stories I've ever heard is that of John Wesley and his brother, founders of Methodism. They were great revivalists in England and the United States a hundred and fifty years ago. The revival that started in England was so great that it swept through that nation, crossed the seas, and caught fire in America. The Wesleys turned the world upside down with the gospel. Their spiritual roots included a background in a large family where the Bible was read together as a family for an hour each day. Then the family members prayed together.

Nothing kept Mrs. Wesley from praying over her children daily. Some of those children turned out to be more motivated for God than the others, but two of the brothers shook the world of their day and made a great mark upon history. Why is that?

Because, as children, the Word of God was sown faithfully into their lives. The Word got in them, took root, budded, and produced fruit.

Something happens when the Word of God gets inside you! Your thoughts change. Your ways change. You're no longer the same. You go up higher.

Answers in the Word

Every problem has an answer in the Word of God. When we get the revelation of that, we have what we need for every circumstance we'll ever face in life. There is virtually no problem that cannot be overcome if we'll just outgrow it. Every Word has a divine purpose attached to it, and every Word has been targeted by God to perform a certain task. As we study the Word to find the right scriptural answer for the problem we face, we can apply that Word to the problem and thereby overcome it. We outgrow it and move on to the next level with God.

If we'll just let the Scripture rain upon us, it will start germinating faith and vision inside us. Then, instead of the devil overcoming our lives, we overcome him with the blood and the word of our testimony—which is filled with the Word of God.

So do you want to prosper? Let the Word of God fall on you, which states, *Beloved, I wish above all things that thou mayest prosper and be in health, even as thy soul prospereth* (3 John 2). Yes, God wants you to prosper! I can show it to you again and again in Scripture. God wants you to prosper!

He's saying, "As My Word falls on you, I'm going to anoint you and cause the fruit of the Spirit to come forth on the inside of you. And if you will be faithful to change your ways—to learn to tithe and give good offerings, cheerfully and willingly—I'm going to allow you to become one of My end-time reapers, one who will be responsible for bringing many men, women, and children throughout the planet to the saving knowledge of Me."

Warnings from the Word of God

As I have already stated, the Word of God is very specifically targeted to produce specific results in our lives. It is filled with promises. It is also filled with warnings. Consider Proverbs 11:24: *There is that scattereth, and yet increaseth; and there is that withholdeth more than is meet, but it tendeth to poverty.* The Living Bible states that the one who holds back more than he is supposed to withhold will lose everything. Why would God give us a Scripture verse like that one? So we would take heed and not lose everything He has blessed us with. He's telling us how to get—and keep—our prosperity. He is telling us how to avoid lack in every area of our lives.

What does that verse mean—*There is that scattereth, and yet increaseth?* That just doesn't make sense in the natural. But we've just seen how God's ways are not our ways: they are higher. This is one of those ways. The natural realm is completely ruled by the spirit realm. The natural realm is where spiritual men and women like you and me must reside—yet we must operate in the spirit realm in order to bring God's will to bear in the natural. As we bring the Word to bear in the spirit realm upon the natural realm, we operate on divine spiritual policy instead of on demonic, fallen spiritual policy. That has no further power over us, once we discover that the things of God's kingdom are in force and operating on our behalf to cause the natural realm to conform to the spiritual.

Until men know God, the Bible says their eyes are so blinded that they do not understand spiritual things. Though many people exert good discipline in their lives and operate on spiritual laws without understanding, they still do not necessarily know what they're doing in the spirit realm. It takes a revelation of Jesus Christ as Savior and the power of the Holy Spirit in order to do that.

When you and I understand the spirit realm and begin to operate in it, especially in the area of finances, we'll see abundance manifested in the natural realm in our lives. So we need to find scriptures dealing with that, then stand on them. We need to study them and learn to live on the level of those scriptures. Because if we do that, the Word will not return to the Lord void. It will accomplish all that He has planned for it to accomplish. It will bring to pass those things in our lives that He has purposed—including abundant prosperity.

Ask God for a heart for souls

Now, as I've already stated, world evangelism costs money. As you repent of not tithing and giving your gifts, God will let His Word rain on you and cause your thinking processes to change. He'll release in you His thoughts regarding tithes and offerings, and reveal to you the truth of scriptures like Luke 6:38: *Give, and it shall be given unto you; good measure, pressed down, and shaken together, and running over, shall men give into your bosom. For with the same measure that ye mete withal it shall be measured to you again.* The Lord will reveal to you that when you give, He causes what you have given to return unto you in so many blessings that you cannot even comprehend it all. Why? Because He just wants to bless you!

God's thoughts are not our thoughts, and one of those divine thoughts was for the eternal salvation of man. That's why much of His Word has to do with His Son: *For God so loved the world, that he gave his only begotten Son, that whosoever believeth in him should not perish, but have everlasting life* (John 3:16). We need a revelation of that same heart. We need to pray, "God, give me Your heart for hurting humanity! Give me Your heart for souls!"

Godly heads of households

This is a word to you men out there: God has placed a mandate upon you to lead your families in righteousness and serving God...taking the oversight in a loving, godly manner. He wants to direct your family *through you* in such a way that it will bring forth the kingdom of God on earth. He has placed a mandate upon your head, as head of your household, to walk in love and wisdom and to rise up and lead your family in the ways of righteousness. And tithing is one of those ways. As I began to study the life of Jacob, I saw clearly that the moment he consecrated himself at Bethel and built "the house of God," he was blessed. From that moment, he became a tither—and from that moment, his household was multiplied.

Listen, friend, you are mandated to be a leader for your wife, your children, your church, and your community. You need to be one who sits down and says, "Let us reason together. We'll tithe. We'll give our offerings. We'll activate the blessings of God in our lives, and we'll move that curse off our families. Then we will be in line for the blessings of God to flow into our lives like milk and honey."

And now I want to speak to those women who are divorced, whose husbands have died, or who have never married. Ma'am, you are now the head of your own household. God has appointed you at this time in your life to walk in that authority. If you are in that position, God will grace you for that. He will lead you to make wise, godly decisions. If you desire to marry, I'll believe with you for the Holy Ghost-filled man you desire to enter your life. Thank God for Holy Ghost men and women who will rise to the occasion, surround all their fears with the Word of God, and knock down the walls of all opposing forces. These are men and women who, once that's done, will give God His portion and go on in to possess the land of abundance in this lifetime.

Now, men and women of faith in every generation have faced those faith barriers. As far back as Abraham, in Genesis 14, there were barriers to faith and battles to fight in order to cross over to the other side. When Abraham tithed to Melchizadek and received a blessing, the king of Sodom immediately appeared to try to talk him out of his blessing. And fear came upon him. This is nothing new. Melchizadek was a type of Christ. Some theologians actually believe that Melchizadek *was* Jesus, but I do not believe that personally, simply because I have found evidence to the contrary in the Word of God. I believe he was a priest and king, but not Jesus. He was, however, a type of Jesus, and he brought out bread and wine to seal the covenant that took place between himself and Abraham.

What do bread and wine signify? Jesus' body and blood. And there in Genesis, five hundred years before the crucifixion is scheduled to take place, we see the first communion being served—to Abraham!

Melchizadek is also representative of the Most High God. When he met Abraham, his name was still Abram. Abram was a man who had just started to develop in his faith. But then he made that huge offering to the king—that tithe to Melchizadek—and that broke something loose over him that began to multiply both his faith and his fortune. When Melchizadek met Abram, he saw something in him that was unique only unto himself. It was greatness recognizing the potential of greatness. Here were two faith guys meeting for the first time—the lesser being blessed by the greater. As Abram was being blessed by Melchizadek, he presented the tithe to the king. Abram didn't even know what was going on. He'd never paid a tithe on anything before. And this tithe represented a lot of money—perhaps as much as a hundred thousand dollars, maybe more. Nevertheless, he did it by faith. Here was a man who was used to gathering and keeping what he gathered—lands, flocks, and spoils of battle. Now he was giving part of it away—ten percent, to be exact. Then he and the king took communion. Abram had just defied his own nature, defeated his own fears.

Then here came the king of Sodom, ready to put a head trip on Abram. Here we see a type of the devil. And who is it that immediately comes and tries to talk us out of tithing, once we commit to tithing faithfully? The king of Sodom represents every fear, every anxiety, every excuse we can think of for not tithing. He is greed incarnate. He is control incarnate. He is negativity incarnate. And he is still on earth today, coming against the things of God with his lies and reasons.

So every man and woman of God on earth today must fight him off, just as Abram did, until they break through those walls of Jericho to enter that Promised Land. Every time a man or woman tithes, the devil will rise up five or ten minutes later, asking questions like, "Why didn't you keep that money for yourself? You earned it! Why didn't you keep it and do your own thing with it?" Sound familiar? I call that the voice of deception. Have you ever heard it?

Because our kingdom is not of this world, our kingdom rules are beyond reason. And God will bless us as we obey them. God's supply is endless on our behalf, and there is always more where that came from. You need to learn to put down the voice of deception—dating back as far as the king of Sodom—in order to press through to your breakthrough. Once you do, you'll reach the point of multiplication and blessing. But if you don't, you'll never enter into what God has for you. That just won't happen until you develop the heart for tithing.

How to get the heart for tithing

As I have already stated, the devil *will* try to come and talk you out of tithing. He did it to Abram—and He'll do it to you. He'll come and whisper, "You can't afford it! What about the bills?"

If you listen, you are letting the devil rob your soul. You are letting him talk you into robbing God—and because of it, you are missing incredible blessings.

When the devil comes and tries to pull that stuff on you, get up in his face and say, "Devil, you can't have my blessing! You can't have my family! You can't have my finances. And you can't have me!" At some point, you're going to have to talk back to that lying voice on the inside of you, and you're going to have to hold the line once you do it. You're going to have to respond like Abram did, in Genesis 14:22-24: *And Abram said to the king of Sodom, I have lift up mine hand unto the Lord, the most high God, the possessor of heaven and earth, that I will not take from a thread even to a shoelatchet, and that I will not take any thing that is thine, lest thou shouldest say, I have made Abram rich: save only that which the young men have eaten....*

Then, in chapter 15, after Abram had given his first tithe, we see that the king of Sodom tried to use spiritual-sounding things to move Abram off what he had just agreed to do, but God assured Abram: *After these things the word of the Lord came unto Abram in a vision, saying, Fear not, Abram...* (v.1). Abram had just given away a mega-sum of money. Why wouldn't he be afraid? But God says, "Don't be afraid! I'm going to come through for you!" I can just hear God talking to Abram. At the end of verse one, the Lord uttered these classic words: *Fear not, Abram: I am thy shield, and thy exceeding great reward.* In *Strong's Concordance,* that word *exceeding* is a beautiful word. In the Hebrew, it means "speedily increasing." So in essence, God is saying, "I am your *speedily increasing* great reward." While Abram was still fighting off those thoughts that not only should he not have tithed, but that he should forget his oath and never again tithe, the Lord said to him in a vision, "Fear not—I am your speedily increasing great reward!" Powerful!

That turned everything around for Abram. That's why he's considered by many today to be the father of faith. He believed God. He stood fast. He not only received his promised and expected reward from God, but he pointed the way for us to do the same. God will speedily increase us. I get excited when I think about that. Don't you?

But something extraordinary happened on the inside of Abram when he finally broke through. Once it dawned on him that God had promised to increase him and that He was a God who could not lie, Abram began to remind God of all sorts of things he had need of. He reminded Him, "Lord, I am childless. I don't have a child, but I will believe You for one." And God said, "All right, you can have a child too."

And right there, even though he was already ninety-nine years old, Abram began to lay claim to the child his wife, Sarai, would one day bear. Abram was saying, *Lord God, what wilt thou give me, seeing I go childless...?* (v.2).

Then verses 4 and 5 state: *And, behold, the word of the Lord came unto him, saying, This shall not be thine heir; but he that shall come forth out of thine own bowels shall be thine heir. And he brought him forth....*

And verse 6 says, *And he believed in the Lord; and he counted it to him for righteousness.* First, Abram believed God with his money. Then his faith became activated, and he could take the biggest leap of faith of all—to believe God for a child in his old age. But it all started with his money.

In chapter 17, verses 1 and 2, God told Abram, "I will bless you all the days of your life." *And when Abram was ninety years old and nine, the Lord appeared to Abram, and said unto him, I am the Almighty God; walk before me, and be thou perfect. And I will make my covenant between me and thee, and will multiply thee exceedingly.* God was saying, "I am not just your financial reward. I will bless you exceedingly in everything you desire." Abram was already ninety-nine years old, and God was still blessing him. In fact, He was getting ready to bless him with the child He promised.

If you desire something in your heart that's from God, it's possible. He can perform that blessing and bring your heart's desire into reality.

So God blessed Abram. And Abram took that same principle and taught it to his children, who taught it to their children. We are learning it today, as the children of Abram—now Abraham—adopted, by faith, now that we are born again.

In Genesis 26:1, we see how important it was that Abraham taught his children the principle of tithing: *And there was a famine in the land, beside the first famine that was in the days of Abraham. And Isaac went unto Abimelech king of the Philistines....* Then verses 12-16 state: *Then Isaac sowed in that land, and received in the same year an hundredfold: and the Lord blessed him. And the man waxed great, and went forward, and grew until he became very great: for he had possession of flocks, and possession of herds, and great store of servants: and the Philistines* [the world] *envied him. For all the wells which his father's servants had digged in the days of Abraham his father, the Philistines had stopped them, and filled them with earth. And Abimelech said unto Isaac, Go from us; for thou art much mightier than we.* Isaac had just demonstrated the same principle of faith taught to him by his daddy. And even in a time of famine, God blessed him. As he sowed, he reaped in the same year herds, houses, and flocks. As everything began to multiply in Isaac's life, the Philistines saw it and were amazed.

Isaac taught the principle of tithing to his son, Jacob. But it took some time for Jacob to cease from operating by what I call "inherited faith," and to start developing faith of his own. Inherited faith is fine. It provides a foundation. But there comes a time in each of our lives when we need to get out there and acquire some faith of our own, for ourselves. No longer is it all right to ride on the coattails of Daddy's faith or Mama's faith or Grandma's faith. We need our own faith, and that's what happened to Jacob out there on the desert floor as that wonderful ladder appeared to him in vision form during the night. He saw the angels ascending and descending before God, and it hit him—God became personal to him right there at that moment. And the first thing he did was promise to give God the tithe. As his father and grandfather before him had promised to give God the tithe, so did Jacob. And from that moment forward, he was blessed. Previously, Jacob had operated on inherited faith. But that night out in the middle of the desert, the revelation that passed down to him became his own.

The moment this principle becomes *rhema* to you—the moment you get a personal revelation of what it means to tithe and give offerings to God—is the moment you will begin to receive your exceeding great reward.

If you don't have a heritage of faith out there in front of you, start one. Right now. It's not too late. Talk about the things of God with your children. Pray together. Develop a heart for tithing. You don't know how to get it? You pray to get it. Right now, pray: *My daddy didn't know You, Lord, but I know You. I never knew about tithing. It was never present in our household. But I intend to be a tither. Help me to faithfully give ten percent of all I have to You, as firstfruits. Reveal to me what You would have me give to You above that. Bless me, Lord, that I may develop a heart for tithing. Bless me, Lord, that I may pass this godly heritage on to my children. In Jesus' name, I pray. Amen!*

Start where you are

When Jacob vowed to tithe before the Lord, he had nothing to give but his word. He started right where he was, and God took him to where He wanted him to be. Jacob, empty-handed, said to God, "I give You my heart, Lord. Here's my pledge: As You give to me, I will surely give a tenth unto You."

We see in Genesis 32 that God immediately set to work to do His part. Everything Jacob touched, from that day forward, appeared to be blessed. In chapter 30, verses 41-43, we read: *And it came to pass, whensoever the stronger cattle did conceive, that Jacob laid the rods before the eyes of the cattle in the gutters, that they might conceive among the rods. But when the cattle were feeble, he put them not in: so the feebler were Laban's, and the stronger Jacob's. And the man increased exceedingly, and had much cattle, and maidservants, and menservants, and camels, and asses.*

So you see, you can start right where you are. Give God your heart. Give Him your pledge. Then as He increases you, keep your word to Him. Then watch what He'll do in your life as He increases you again and again. That may not happen on the first day, and perhaps not even on the second day. It may not happen until you become full of the Word of God and get that *rhema* understanding of what it means to serve God by faith with your tithes and offerings, but it will come. Trust me—it will come.

That day will come when the walls fall down, making the way for you to walk right into the Promised Land and possess it for yourself. Then as God blesses you and multiplies you, continue to walk in the light of Proverbs 3:9,10: *Honour the Lord with thy substance, and with the firstfruits of all thine increase: So shall thy barns be filled with plenty, and thy presses shall burst out with new wine.*

Epilogue

Have you learned anything from these Scripture principles I have just shared with you? I pray your answer will be "yes." If you are a faithful tither and giver of offerings to the work of Jesus Christ on earth today, I pray that God will richly bless and multiply you according to His Word.

If you are not currently tithing but are a born-again believer, will you consider praying with me? *Lord, I realize I have not been faithful in tithing and giving gifts to You. I did not fully understand what the Scriptures had to say on this important subject. But I desire to be a faithful tither, and so I repent today of not tithing and ask You to help me develop faithfulness in this area of giving. Please give me the heart of the Father where tithing is concerned, and give me a heart for souls. In Jesus' name, I pray. Amen.*

If you are not yet a believer but would like to receive Jesus Christ as your Lord and Savior, will you pray with me? *Dear Jesus, I come to You a sinner who is willing to repent of my sins. I ask You to forgive me and cleanse me of my sins. At the same time, I willingly forgive all those who have hurt or offended or wounded me. I ask that You enter my heart today and set up your kingdom as my Lord and Savior. Fill me with the Holy Spirit, and direct my life. In Jesus' name, I pray. Amen.*

If you have just prayed either one of these prayers, I'd like to hear from you. Please write me at:

Walter Hallam
Abundant Life Christian Center
P.O. Box 1515
La Marque, Texas 77568

Please know that Cindy and I and the congregation at Abundant Life Christian Center in La Marque, Texas, are praying for you! God bless you mightily as you apply these scripture principles for prosperous living to your daily lives.

WALTER HALLAM MINISTRIES

BOOKS

A CITY CALLED HEAVEN	$5.95
DELIVERED FROM DEPRESSION	5.95
DELIVERED FROM INIQUITIES	5.95
BORN AGAIN	4.95
UNDERSTANDING TONGUES	4.95
DON'T LOOK BACK	4.95
GOD IS MORE THAN ENOUGH	4.95
THE RAPTURE	4.95
WHAT IS PROSPERITY AND DOES GOD WANT YOU TO HAVE IT?	9.95

SINGLE TAPES

(101)	RECESSION PROOF YOUR HOME	$5.00
(102)	LOAVES AND FISHES	5.00
(103)	RAPTURE	5.00
(104)	BORN AGAIN	5.00
(105)	THE LOCAL CHURCH	5.00
(106)	HEALING	5.00
(107)	FREE FROM INIQUITY	5.00
(108)	UNDERSTANDING THE DIVERSITY OF TONGUES	5.00
(109)	PRAYERS THAT GET ANSWERS	5.00
(110)	THE TRUTH ABOUT HALLOWEEN	5.00
(112)	GET HEALED	5.00
(113)	MAKING GODLY DECISIONS	5.00

TWO-TAPE SERIES

(202)	FAITH THAT OVERCOMES THE FACTS	$10.00
(203)	MORE THAN A CONQUEROR	10.00
(204)	OVERCOMING HINDRANCES	10.00
(205)	THE POWER OF THE RESURRECTION & BLOOD	10.00
(206)	PREPARING FOR THE MOVE OF GOD	10.00

THREE-TAPE SERIES

(301)	ANOINTING OF THE SPIRIT	$15.00
(302)	CHANGED INTO HIS IMAGE	15.00
(303)	HOW TO BE HEALED FROM OFFENSE FOREVER	15.00

FOUR-TAPE SERIES

(401)	REDEEMED FROM THE CURSE OF POVERTY	$20.00
(402)	HEARING THE VOICE OF GOD	20.00
(403)	KEEP YOUR HEALING	20.00
(404)	AUTOMATIC WEAPONS OF GOD	20.00
(405)	RENEWING YOUR MIND	20.00
(406)	UNDERSTANDING THE MINISTRY OF HELPS	20.00
(407)	LEARN HOW TO OVERCOME DEPRESSION	20.00

SIX-TAPE SERIES

(601)	BREAKING THE SPIRIT OF POVERTY	$30.00
(602)	WORKING OF SPIRIT IN LOCAL CHURCH	30.00
(603)	UNDERSTANDING THE END TIMES	30.00
(604)	OVERCOMING CHAMPIONS	30.00

SEVEN-TAPE SERIES

(701)	CRUSADE FOR THE FAMILY	$35.00

EIGHT-TAPE SERIES

(801)	KEYS TO THE KINGDOM	$40.00
(802)	THE ROAD TO GREAT FAITH	40.00
(803)	YOU CAN HAVE A GODLY MARRIAGE	40.00
(804)	COVENANT FAMILY	40.00

TWELVE-TAPE SERIES

(1201)	WHY GOD WANTS YOU TO PROSPER	$60.00
(1202)	VICTORIOUS CHRISTIAN FAMILY	60.00

Add 15% for Shipping and Handling

**Mail request to:
Walter Hallam Ministries
P.O. Box 1515 • La Marque, TX 77568**